Madison's
HERITAGE
REDISCOVERED

Fred Engle
Robt. Grise
Kathy Engle

D1607493

Madison's HERITAGE REDISCOVERED

Stories from a Historic Kentucky County

Dr. Fred A. Engle Jr. & Dr. Robert N. Grise

Edited by KATHRYN ENGLE

Charleston   London

THE
History
PRESS

Published by The History Press
Charleston, SC 29403
www.historypress.net

Unless otherwise noted, all photos are courtesy of the Eastern Kentucky University Library
Special Collections and Archives.

First published 2012

Manufactured in the United States

ISBN 978.1.60949.627.2

Library of Congress CIP data applied for.

Notice: The information in this book is true and complete to the best of our knowledge. It is
offered without guarantee on the part of the authors or The History Press. The authors and
The History Press disclaim all liability in connection with the use of this book.

Dedicated to the memory of Dr. and Mrs. Fred A. Engle Sr.
and Dr. and Mrs. P.M. Grise, who began this Madison County journey.

CONTENTS

CONTENTS

ACKNOWLEDGEMENTS

Many people have given their time, effort and knowledge in support of *Madison's Heritage Rediscovered*. Dr. Engle would like to thank his wife, Mary, for all her help and support. Dr. Grise would like to thank his wife, Martha, for her support and editing. Kathryn would like to thank Dr. Linda Frost, director of the EKU Honors Program, and Dr. Alan Banks, director of the EKU Center for Appalachian Studies, for their support and encouragement of this project.

The authors and editor would like to thank Eastern Kentucky University for all the opportunities the school has provided them and the *Richmond Register* for supplying the platform for these articles. The authors would like to thank the staff of the EKU Library Special Collections and Archives (archives. eku.edu), especially Jackie Couture, whose expertise and knowledge of the county was invaluable to this project. Thanks also to the countless friends and family members who have made this book possible.

INTRODUCTION

Local history can be found in many places: the bottom of desk drawers, in libraries and archives and in the memories of longtime community residents. History is often discovered, lost, then rediscovered as generations of people look for their heritage and their community's past.

Madison's Heritage Rediscovered is the product of such a search for community history. It is the culmination of hundreds of hours of research, writing, energy and pride in the history of Madison County, Kentucky. The authors, Dr. Fred A. Engle Jr. and Dr. Robert N. Grise, have devoted more than forty years to the preservation and continuation of their county's heritage through their weekly newspaper column, Madison's Heritage. This book is but a small glimpse into their large body of work chronicling Madison's past.

Madison County has a rich history of pioneer settlement, education and local and national leadership. Located in the Bluegrass region of central Kentucky at the foothills of the Appalachian Mountains, Madison County was formed in 1786 from Lincoln County, Virginia. It features rolling hills and fertile farmland, is bounded on the north by the Kentucky River and is bisected by Interstate 75. The location of Daniel Boone's pioneer fort and site of numerous historical events, including the Battle of Richmond, the county is known for its many prominent citizens, businesses, civic organizations and institutions.

Richmond, the county seat, is Madison's largest city and home to Eastern Kentucky University (EKU). The Blue Grass Army Depot occupies a large portion of central Madison County, and the city of Berea, home to progressive Berea College, sits at the southern edge of the county. Smaller communities scattered throughout the county have also

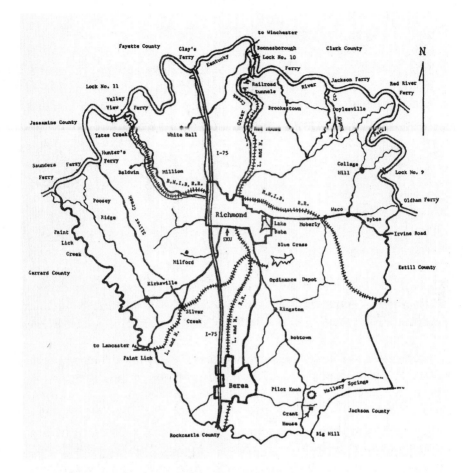

A map of Madison County, Kentucky, by Dr. Robert N. Grise.

played a large role in the development of the area. Many significant and unique features of the county's past have provided plenty of interesting subject matter for the authors.

My whole life, I had known that my grandfather wrote a column about Madison County history for our local newspaper, the *Richmond Register*. It was not until I was in college that I realized the significance of his and his coauthor's contributions to the county. Through their preservation efforts and writings over the years, they have shared the history of Madison County with residents of all generations. Since 1969, they have published over 2,000 articles, as well as three earlier compilations of articles, and continue to share their knowledge of local history to readers every week.

Many characteristics make the Madison's Heritage column special. The articles cover a wide range of subject matter, from the pioneer history of the county to stories about local people, businesses, places and events. Many different sources have been used over the years—historic documents, archival materials, old newspapers, items and accounts from community members and even the authors own memories of growing up in Richmond. In addition, the column's duration and volume, as well as the depth and quality of the articles, are exceptional. Madison's Heritage has given readers unprecedented insights into the county's past through its extensive supply of local history, uncovering many hidden reserves of information and helping further define the county's past.

Out of pure love for local history and without academic backgrounds in history, the authors have worked tirelessly researching Madison's past, using their skills as writers to bring public history alive. Their remarkably similar lives are often reflected in their articles, and their experiences as lifelong residents of the county provide a unique perspective on bygone times.

Madison's Heritage is an interactive, collaborative effort between the authors and the community, as the authors continue to produce articles weekly and the community continues to be interested and involved. The column has incorporated comments, suggestions, inquiries, materials and facts provided by local citizens, producing a community history with the contributions of countless Madison Countians interested in preserving their heritage.

As a senior in the Honors Program at EKU, I began a multifaceted project involving the Madison's Heritage column. In my research, I found articles in my grandpa's desk drawers and in the EKU Library Special Collections and Archives and set out to compile, catalog and digitize all of the Madison's Heritage articles. I also talked to the authors to get their perspective on their work and our community's past. As daunting as this task proved to be, I was constantly rewarded with new knowledge and further appreciation for my grandpa's work and my county. I wanted the articles I digitized to be widely and easily accessible, so I created the Madison's Heritage Online website (madisonsheritage.omeka.net) to house the articles and information about the column. I also wrote a thesis on the column and its significance to the county based on my research.

Madison's Heritage Rediscovered is the final piece of my project and another chapter in the history of the Madison's Heritage column. With the input of the authors, I selected and edited over sixty articles from the column originally published in the *Richmond Register*. It was extremely difficult to

Madison's Heritage articles have appeared weekly in the *Richmond Register* since April 1969.

choose articles from a weekly collection spanning from 1969 to the present. Many intriguing stories were left out of this particular compilation but may be found on the Madison's Heritage website. Some articles were edited more heavily than others, but efforts were made to preserve the integrity, style and voice of the authors, as well as the factual accuracy of the information. This book is not meant to be a comprehensive or academic history of the county but rather a collection of short vignettes of the lives of Madison Countians that aims to reflect the focus, variety and research interests of the Madison's Heritage authors.

Madison's Heritage Rediscovered commemorates Drs. Engle and Grise's contributions to local history and their legacy of decades of dedication, scholarship and curiosity. As the Madison's Heritage column has done for decades, it is my hope that this book will foster interest in the fascinating history of Madison County and inspire further exploration and enjoyment of the area's rich heritage.

So start looking in old desk drawers, check out the library archives and seek out local memory-keepers and elderly residents to find out more about your community's past. Dig up your family history, ask questions, seek answers and keep persevering.

I hope you enjoy rediscovering Madison's Heritage as much as I have.

—Kathryn Engle

EARLY MADISON COUNTY

THE KENTUCKY FRONTIER

Robert Grise

Let's go back and take a look at the early history of this area that we call Madison County.

The oldest inhabitants were probably the Native Americans, who were nomadic hunters, gatherers and fishers who built what are known as pre-Indian mounds. It has been written that Madison County is one of the richest in the state in regard to prehistoric burial and ceremonial places. Indian Fort Mountain, three miles east of Berea, is one such site.

The Indians, misnamed because explorers thought that they had landed in India, were here around AD 1500. While few lived here permanently, this area is where the Shawnee, Cherokee and Wyandotte tribes hunted, fished, traded and fought with each other.

In 1769, Daniel Boone and a group of explorers, including his brother, Squire, entered this area. In the spring of 1770, Squire returned to North Carolina for more supplies, leaving Daniel all alone. One of the explorers had been killed by wolves, and others had been captured or slain by Native Americans. When Squire returned, Daniel was not at the campsite in the southeastern portion of what is now Madison County. Squire cut his name and the date, 1770, on a large stone, which had fallen from a hillside for Daniel to see and then went looking for his brother. That stone is now in the lobby of the Madison County Courthouse.

The Round Hill mound near Kirksville, shown in this photo taken in the 1890s, is one of the most well-known mounds in the county.

The Squire Boone Rock, as it has come to be known, was moved from its original location in the southeastern part of the county and put on display outside the Madison County Courthouse until the 1960s, when it was moved inside and put under glass.

The Boones reunited and returned a few years later with other pioneers, blazing the Wilderness Road (also known as the Wilderness Trail or Boone's Trace). Even though there were about a dozen Native American tribes that hunted, traded and planted maize here, it was the Cherokee that made a deal with a North Carolina land development company named the Transylvania Company. Daniel Boone helped with the negotiations as an agent of the company in 1775. The Transylvania Company traded the Cherokee $50,000 worth of merchandise for 20 million acres of land in the vast region of Kentucky, generally between the present cities of Nashville, Tennessee, and Cincinnati, Ohio.

Daniel Boone and others were hired to set up a colony. Boone and his fellow pioneers built a little fort at the mouth of Otter Creek in what is now northern Madison County. They then built a large fort, Fort Boonesborough, near the Kentucky River, close to where Boonesborough State Park is now located.

The settlers established a government and passed several laws. When they sent representatives to the nation's capitol to get chartered, the Virginia government said that Boone had had no right to make a deal with the Cherokee, so they disallowed the land claims of the pioneers and changed the name of this area from Transylvania to Kentucky County, Virginia. Because most settlers were illiterate and spelling was not as exact in the eighteenth century, the Native-American name "Kentucky" was spelled many different ways, such as "Kaintuck" or "Kentuckie." Just think, if Virginia hadn't done that, we would now be living in Madison County, Transylvania!

BOONESBOROUGH: MADISON COUNTY'S PIONEER TOWN

Robert Grise

Newer residents of Madison County may wonder about all the interest in Fort Boonesborough. After all, isn't it just another fort? No, Boonesborough and Fort Harrod at Harrodsburg were the first two settlements west of the Appalachian Mountains. Connected by the Wilderness Road blazed by pioneers led by Daniel Boone, these two first forts were stopover stations for thousands of settlers coming from North Carolina into this unspoiled and fertile area, where a family could have a farm for practically nothing

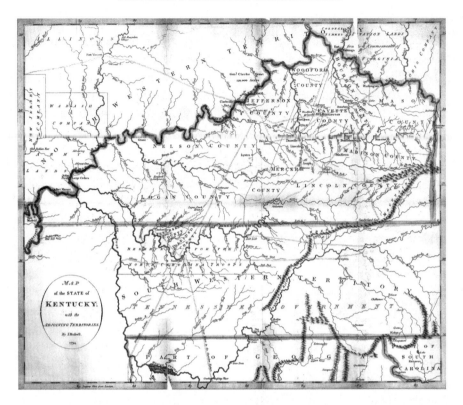

Pioneers traveled the Wilderness Road into Kentucky through the Cumberland Gap, making their way north to Boonesborough and on to the west. This 1794 map shows the path of the pioneers and the changing boundaries of Madison County.

except their hard work. Several hundred thousand persons came over the Wilderness Road through the Cumberland Gap from 1775 through the 1790s, and the fort at Boonesborough was something of a motel with many travelers staying a short while and then moving on farther west to get inexpensive lands.

Boonesborough set a number of "firsts" for the area: it was the first seat of government west of the Appalachian Mountains; passed the first laws; held the first formal religious service; was the first town to be incorporated in Kentucky (County, Virginia); and had the first ferry, the first wharf and even the first warehouse for shipping hides, tobacco and corn down the river.

Among the many attacks and skirmishes at Boonesborough was the big siege in 1778. For nine days, the fort residents successfully defended themselves from Indian attacks, helping to secure the western frontier from Indian and British domination.

In October 1779, some four years after Boone's first fort was built, the town of Boonesborough on the Kentucky River was chartered by the Virginia State Legislature. You will remember that Kentucky did not become a separate state until 1792. Petition for a charter was made by Richard Calloway, Daniel Boone and the men of the Bradley, Estill, Gass, Kennedy, Powell, Taylor, Thurston and Rollins families.

Twenty acres were divided into half-acre lots, and streets were laid out. An additional 50 lots were directed to be marked off, and 570 acres, the balance of the total 640 acres, were to be established as a "commons" for the grazing of livestock, militia drilling and other uses. The "commons" of the fort was where Richard Calloway and other pioneers who had been killed by the Indians were buried.

Lots were at first to be conveyed to persons making applications on a "first come, first served" basis, with the condition that within three years the owner of the lot would build a dwelling house at least sixteen by sixteen feet with a brick, stone or mud-brick chimney. Many of the lots were awarded by lottery while others were sold for fifty cents to a dollar. By 1789, the town of Boonesborough had over a hundred houses and was quite a commercial center. It had stores, a post office, warehouses, taverns, blacksmiths, rooming houses, firearm dealers and a lot of farmers and hunters.

Notes on Pioneer Times

Fred Engle and Robert Grise

The first cabin in Madison County outside the fort at Boonesborough was built in 1775 by Squire Boone. Daniel's brother had about 1,000 acres on Silver Creek and called his land Stockfield. Henderson and Company opened the first store in Kentucky at Boonesborough in April of 1775, selling lead, powder and other goods. In May of 1775, the white population of Kentucky was around 300, all living within 50 miles of Boonesborough. Some 230 acres were under cultivation in corn. Joseph Doniphan taught the first school in the county at Boonesborough in 1779. He averaged seventeen students. The first minister authorized to marry people was Reverend James Haw (1786). The first group of Dutch in Kentucky settled at White Oak Spring Station on the Kentucky River, one mile above Boonesborough in 1781. In the 1780s, General Green Clay built the first hewed log house in the county at the present location of White Hall, the home of Cassius M. Clay.

Although corn was the big crop in Madison County in the early days, pioneers also planted other produce. John Boyle planted peach stones in 1775 and, in 1776, Richard Hinde raised watermelons and muskmelons. James Bridges had a turnip patch and Nathaniel Hart grew pumpkins. This pumpkin patch was near Estill's Station (Fort Estill) and near the Wilderness Road and the travelers soon began calling the area Pumpkin Run, a name still heard today, along with the picturesque Cow Bell Hollow.

The original Madison County covered over three million acres in an area about 50 by 100 miles, with one corner extending clear to the state line in southeastern Kentucky. In 1780, Virginia made Fayette, Jefferson and Lincoln Counties out of Kentucky County, Virginia. In 1784, Nelson was created and then, in 1786, Mercer and Madison were made out of Lincoln County. For about half a dozen years, this was Madison County, Virginia. The Madison County Court was organized in 1786, and a stone combination courthouse and jail was built at the little village of Milford.

The site of Daniel Boone's pioneer town is now a state park, complete with a re-created fort and yearly reenactments of the Siege of Boonesborough. The park offers many events and recreational activities throughout the year.

After it lost its bid to be the capital city of Kentucky in 1792 and after many residents had moved on westward or to other Kentucky cities such as Lexington, Boonesborough began to dwindle away. So many people left by 1820 that there was not much of any town remaining. The post office, which had stayed open to serve farmers in that area of the county, was finally discontinued in 1866.

ADVENTURES OF EARLY EXPLORERS

Fred Engle

Daniel Boone was not the first white man to come to Kentucky. Among others, John Findley (sometimes spelled Finley) had been to Kentucky in 1754. When Boone and Findley were with Major General Braddock fighting the French and Indians in 1755, Findley regaled Boone with stories of Kentucky and how to get there through the Cumberland Gap and how to follow the Warriors' Path to Ohio. The land was fertile and the deer and buffalo plentiful.

In May of 1769, a group of explorers including Boone, Findley, Joseph Monay, William Cool, Joseph Holden and Boone's brother-in-law, John Stuart, started out from Carolina, going over the Blue Ridge, Stone Mountain, Iron Mountain and across Holston Valley and the Clinch River. At Powell's Valley they picked up a hunter's trail that led them through the Cumberland Gap to the Warriors' Path. They finally camped at Round Stone Lick Fork on the west branch of the Rockcastle River.

Boone wanted to see the meadows of Kentucky, so he climbed to a high ridge between the Rockcastle and Kentucky Rivers and looked over into what is now Madison and Garrard counties. It was his first sight of our county where he was to build his fort. Warriors' Path led them on across the Kentucky River to the Indian town of Eskippakithiki on the Lulbegrud Creek in what is now Clark County. On June 7, the group made their first base camp—Station Camp Creek.

It was not until December, a few days before Christmas, that Boone and Stuart, who had separated from the rest of the party, ran upon any Indians. A mounted group of Shawnee were on their way home to Ohio (Chillocothe). The Indians forced the men to turn over their skins, guns and horses. They ordered the explorers to go home and leave the Indian hunting ground alone.

Boone and Stuart followed the Indians and stole back four of the horses. The Indians in turn recaptured the horses and took the men captive. They tied them up and took them as far as present day Maysville on the Ohio River. There, Boone and Stuart managed to escape into a cane patch. When they returned to their main camp, they found that the others, including Findley, had left. Boone and Stuart finally caught up with them near the Rockcastle River. This story is just one of the many accounts of the adventures of early explorers in this area.

STATIONS EXISTED BEFORE THERE WAS A MADISON COUNTY

Robert Grise

As settlers came into the Boonesborough area before it was known as Madison County, they traveled to "stations" where they could find food, protection and a safe place to rest. Those early "rest stops" were the pioneers' forerunners of modern motels for travelers.

The earliest stations were fortified and guarded to some extent from Indians and wild animals. Fort Estill, or Estill's Station, was established on the Wilderness Road, the main trail between the Cumberland Gap and Boonesborough. Today, a historical marker along U.S. 25 identifies the approximate location. It was about fifteen miles south of Fort Boonesborough. Another such place was Twetty's Fort, established in 1775, about five miles south of Richmond before Richmond was even a town.

In the early 1800s, these stations were more like a British tavern or inn. According to the nineteenth-century newspaper editor and historian French Tipton, there were two taverns (stations) in the county in 1796 and five more clustered around Milford, which at that time was the county seat.

At those places a traveler could, for a fee, find food, drink, a night's lodging, as well as a stable and oats for his horse. The traveler could also find others who could tell him about local conditions. He could find folks with whom to have conversations or gossip of a political, economic or social nature.

Tipton recorded in his history notes that in these early days one inn had peach brandy for one pound English money. Whiskey went for six pence for a half pint, and meals were one shilling, six pence. In the early 1800s, David C. Irvine and Embry Talton's hotel charged about thirty-seven U.S. cents for dinner or supper. Horses were fed and stabled for a little over twelve cents.

The Richmond Hotel was established in 1816 and was advertised in the newspapers as being "at the sign of George Washington." At that time a lot of settlers could not read or write, and it was common for a tavern to have a sign with the recognizable shape of an animal, Indian symbol or the profile of a famous person.

"Travelers and other visitants are respectfully solicited," an early Richmond Hotel advertisement stated. "They may depend on the promptest attention to render their situation easy."

Buffalo Trails and Creeks

Robert Grise

Animal trails were the first roads in Madison County, so said William Chenault, nineteenth-century Richmond attorney and historian. Chenault's writings about pioneer travel were edited by Dr. J.T. Dorris, professor of history at Eastern, and published in the April 1932 issue of the *Register of the Kentucky Historical Society*.

Before the roads of Madison County were established, Chenault wrote, the well-traveled buffalo trails were used by Native Americans and then the settlers from Virginia and North Carolina. The major trails led from the mouth of Otter Creek to Mulberry Lick and Log Lick on Muddy Creek; from the mouth of Otter Creek up its east fork and Drowning Creek to Big Blue Lick; and from the mouth of Tates Creek to Irvine's Lick near the present site of the city of Richmond.

There were side trails leading off to many of the sulfur licks in the county. Weeds, grass and small brush were kept beaten down by the animals and human travelers, so that even these "side roads" were easily seen and followed. Chenault wrote that by 1784 a large amount of the previously plentiful game had been killed or had left this area. Grass and brush began to grow up along these trails, causing the county to appear more wild and overgrown than it had ten years earlier when the settlers first began to arrive.

The various creeks and branches of Madison County were mostly named by Daniel Boone, Chenault wrote. Streams such as Muddy Creek and Otter Creek were named for their characteristics. Station Camp Creek was in Madison in those early days when the county extended far to the southeast portion of the state. Tates Creek, Jacks Creek, Hines Creek and others were named for early landowners along them.

Dreaming Creek, which begins on the Eastern Kentucky University campus and flows through the eastern portion of Richmond, now mostly underground, was named, it is said, because old Daniel went to sleep by it after working nearby making a trap for bears. He dreamt that he was surrounded by Indians and awoke to discover that it was true. The story goes that Daniel tricked the Indians, telling them that he would go peacefully if they helped him finish his trap. As they helped, Daniel triggered the trap and caught their hands in a split hickory log, giving him time to escape.

THE COUNTY SEAT

Robert Grise

Madison County's first seat of government was a small stone and wood building at Milford, which was roughly in the center of the then much larger county. There was no easy supply of water at Milford, and travel to get there to do legal matters such as recording deeds was long and difficult. The famous 1798 Kennedy-Kerley fistfight in a pen at Milford concerning whether or not the government should be moved to Richmond was good entertainment, but the county court had by that time already voted to move.

Richmond was established as the county seat in 1798, a preemption of John Miller, who owned the land where Richmond now stands. The town was chartered by the state in 1809. The first of three county courthouses was built in the center of this little pioneer village in 1799 by Tyra Rhodes and was said to be near the site of Mt. Nebo, a pioneer church house. Adjacent to the courthouse were the jail (referred to in the early records as the "gaol") and the market house, a long strip of sheds along First Street for farmers to sell their produce. The present day courthouse parking lot at the corner of First and Irvine was the site of at least two hangings during the last half of the nineteenth century.

Although there was a little wooden bridge soon constructed on East Main where it crossed over Dreaming Creek, the streets in those days were little more than improved dirt pathways. Facing the courthouse on Main, First, Second and Irvine Streets were mostly one-story buildings of brick or wood, which housed taverns, stores and craftsmen supplying local needs such as shoes and boots, saddles, harnesses, furniture and pottery. The taverns, which were a combination rooming house, restaurant and saloon, did brisk business on days when court was in session. Most physicians and lawyers operated out of their own homes. In its early years, Richmond became a

This photo from the 1800s shows a typical one-story storefront on Second Street in Richmond. According to French Tipton, all the buildings on First and Second Streets looked like this in the nineteenth century.

place where several lawyers set up office, because of all the early conflicting land claims in the Boonesborough area.

In this little pioneer town there were about three dozen residences, most of wood framing from local sawmills, some built of logs and a few that were native stone or brick. People with money could have things like English dishes and silver imported by wagon from the Northeast. The first school in Richmond was reported by newspaper editor French Tipton as being taught by Israel Donaldson in a small, one-room building at the southeast corner of Main and First Streets in 1799.

THE RICHMOND MARKET

Robert Grise

In the late 1800s, long before the automobile came to Richmond, most travelers from a distance arrived by passenger train or stagecoach. Some came by private or rented buggies and saddle horses. Many residents of

Madison County were in the habit of walking several miles to the county seat. Of course, we could not do that sort of thing now with lines of fast-moving cars and trucks on crowded highways, exhaust fumes and the increased population compared with that of over a century ago.

Richmond was a county court town, with lots of people visiting during the first days of the month when court cases were tried. All sorts of relatives and friends arrived, not only to support their old buddy who was in trouble but also to use this event as an excuse to come and "party" for a few days, especially around the saloons on First Street. Richmond merchants were well aware of the opportunity and had their wares prominently displayed to entice the potential customers to come in and buy. Special sales were announced in the previous week's *Kentucky Register*.

Court days were also local market days. Farmers would bring in all kinds of livestock and produce to sell on First Street beside the courthouse, which had been made wide for that purpose on the very first plats of the town. Nearly every Saturday there were horses, mules, cows and calves, sheep,

This 1917 photo of First Street in Richmond shows men and boys trading horses and mules beside the courthouse on a typical court day.

goats, hogs, geese, turkeys and chickens of various types and sometimes other kinds of animals in the market square. Farmers brought sorghum, homemade preserves, salt pork, hams, shoulders, sausage and corn of various kinds in the wintertime.

In summer, there appeared all kinds of homegrown fruits and vegetables by the basketful. Ladies showed the products of their skills: blankets, quilts, ladies' clothing, sunbonnets, corn-shuck dolls, home remedy medications, homemade candy and other such items. Some operated homemade hot food stands for the crowds. Hunters brought in cured hides of fox, skunk, raccoon, wolf and deer and also cured horse and cowhides. Tack trading was a common thing to see, with saddles, bridles and harnesses sometimes changing hands more than once during the day.

The market square was also a sort of job center. Men who wanted to work as "day laborers" could go hoping to link up with farmers, businessmen or others who needed workers.

Dr. Fred Engle and I can remember the old First Street marketplace in the 1930s; on a Saturday morning, it was crowded thick with people, animals and merchandise from one side to the other, from Main Street to Irvine Street.

REMEMBERING THE BATTLE OF RICHMOND

Fred Engle

Every year, a Civil War reenactment of the Battle of Richmond takes place in late August at the Richmond Battlefield Park on U.S. 421 just south of Richmond. The sponsor, the Battle of Richmond Association, is committed to preserving this important part of Madison County's heritage.

The battle took place on August 29–30, 1862. The fighting went from Kingston through Duncannon Lane and on north to Richmond. It was one of the most decisive Confederate victories of the entire Civil War.

Major General Edmund Kirby Smith led 19,000 southern troops north from Knoxville. Cumberland Gap was occupied by the Federals, so Smith dispatched some troops to keep them in check. Smith's remaining men, totaling about 12,000, proceeded through pro-Union east Tennessee and Kentucky. Smith went through a gap near Barbourville, Kentucky. The area was pro-Union, and guerillas sniped at the troops as they marched through.

Brigadier General Mahlon Manson led an inexperienced group of U.S. troops during the Battle of Richmond. His saber, Colt .36 caliber pistol, wallet, belt buckle and epaulets, which decorated his uniform, are on display at the Battlefield Park Visitors Center outside of Richmond on U.S. 421. *Photo by Kathryn Engle.*

Confederate cavalry defeated a Federal force at Big Hill on August 23rd. Smith's forces had become strung out crossing through the barren and drought-stricken areas of southern Kentucky.

On August 29th, Federal forces, about 3,500 strong under Brigadier General Mahlon Manson, defeated a Confederate cavalry force near Duncannon Lane, with Federal cavalry chasing them to Joe's Lick Knob before falling back after dark.

On the morning of August 30th, Manson's inexperienced Federal recruits were pummeled by Smith's Confederates just south of the Mt. Zion Christian Church, mainly on what is now Blue Grass Army Depot property. People still point out the cannonball damage visible on the south sidewall of the church. Although reinforced by Charles Cruft's regiments arriving from Richmond, the Federal army withdrew in confusion to the Duncannon Lane area.

The Confederates attacked the Federal's left flank around 1:00 p.m. and, after an intense half hour of conflict in the hot afternoon sun, the

Union forces were overtaken, with many soldiers surrendering. The Federals retreated toward Richmond.

Another line of battle was formed in the Richmond Cemetery as General William "Bull" Nelson, the U.S. commander, arrived on the field. Once again the inexperienced U.S. troops were no match for the Confederate forces. It is said that both the Union and Confederate soldiers on that hot August afternoon drank from the cool waters of the Woodlawn spring (but not at the same time), which flowed just across the bypass from where Kroger is currently located.

The Union troops were defeated and those captured were marched to Richmond. The wrought iron fence that surrounded the courthouse served as a jail for the prisoners. This fence now stands at the edge of the Richmond cemetery along East Main Street.

The Confederates went on to take Lexington and Frankfort and even swore in a Confederate governor in mid-September 1862. Another Confederate general, Braxton Bragg, and his army fought at the Battle of Perryville in early October 1862, with some of Smith's men joining the fight. After the battle, Bragg and the southern army withdrew back into Tennessee, and Kentucky was safe for the Union.

A major disappointment to both Smith and Bragg was the failure of Kentucky to rally around the Stars and Bars and officially join the Confederates. Most cheered as the grey army rode by but did not join the ranks. Even so, the Battle of Richmond was a major decisive victory for the Confederates.

WHO STOLE THE HONEY IN 1862?

Robert Grise

"Who stole the honey?" That question arose right after the Civil War Battle of Richmond in 1862. It went unanswered until 1920, some fifty-eight years later.

During the Battle of Richmond, part of the fighting was near the Madison Female Institute campus, now the location of Madison Middle School. When the fighting ended, some of the wounded and dying of both armies were taken to the only handy place—the classroom building of the Female Institute.

Conditions were very bad. Wounded were laid on the floors and teachers and a few students tended to them as best they could without much in the way of medications, bandages, sufficient food or adequate water supply. There were a few physicians, both local and army, who had only a few surgical instruments and limited time to minister to the patients.

There was no pain-relieving anesthesia, so when it was necessary to remove a soldier's badly wounded leg or arm, several persons held the poor fellow down on a table while a physician sawed the limb off. It was later reported in the weekly newspapers that in nearby homes and stores on Main Street, people could sometimes hear the screams of agony.

When the Madison Female Institute closed in 1919, the Richmond Board of Education obtained the campus and buildings, and the public school administration began to renovate the old classroom building. Workers found that on the walls of the Institute building there were eleven layers of wallpaper that had been put on over the years! When the last layer was removed, it was discovered that several wounded soldiers had scribbled notes on the plaster walls. Some were comments on their suffering and some were last messages to loved ones.

One wounded Union soldier, C.D. Henderson of the Forty-Fifth Ohio Volunteer Infantry, wrote his confession on the wall that, even though the food supply was not sufficient, he had stolen a jar of honey and had eaten all of it! At that time the shortage of food for the wounded was a rather serious matter of concern.

Apparently, Henderson waited awhile until he felt safe in writing and signing his confession on the wall, perhaps just before he was moved elsewhere. And, that's who stole the honey.

Madison Countians

Clever Cook's Corn Breads Purchased Freedom for Herself and Her Family

Robert Grise

In the early years of the nineteenth century, there was a public market house, actually a long row of roofed booths along the First Street side of the Madison County Courthouse yard. Persons who had grown or made the products they wanted to sell could rent a booth from the county—some for a day, others for months at a time. There they could compete with others who had everything from pottery, fresh fruits and vegetables in season, dressed chickens and handmade harnesses, to bark baskets, fresh-killed squirrels and rabbits and salt-cured country ham.

There was one exception to the county court rule that you had to have grown or made what you sold in the market house. In the center of that long row was a ten-foot booth operated on weekends and court days for several years by Mammy Lou, John Miller's slave who was the regular cook at Miller's tavern at the corner of First and Main. John Miller was the founder of Richmond and gave the land for the courthouse square.

Mammy Lou was said to have been a physically large woman with much stamina, who split firewood for the stove and cooked wonderful meals for guests at the tavern. She was said to nearly always have a big smile and, according to several items in the old Richmond newspapers, was sometimes called "Mammy Blue" because her skin was said to be so black that in a certain light it had a blue cast.

Mammy Lou was not only strong and skilled in cooking, but she was also smart and ambitious. She persuaded Miller to give her permission to operate her cornmeal booth on weekends, and he even provided her with cooking utensils and her first barrel of cornmeal. Miller allowed Mammy Lou to use all she earned at the market house toward buying freedom from slavery for her two children and herself.

Among the white cornmeal products Mammy Lou became popular for were corn sticks, fritters, muffins, hoecakes, corn pone, egg-batter bread and spoon bread. Old newspaper accounts revealed that folks would gather around her booth just to watch her seemingly magic motions, which produced the delicious corn breads that were so eagerly sought after by the public. There was a pinch of salt, a dab of butter, a sprinkle of sugar, a few drops of molasses and a bit of cinnamon or other spice that in some wonderful way made her fresh hot breads so delicious. It was said that even people who lived in the big houses on West Main and Lancaster Avenue sent for those remarkable breads.

Her outstandingly delicious spoon bread, wrote the 1940s local historian Green Clay, was made in a large pie pan and had both coarse cornmeal and some finely powdered cornmeal, which she made with a mortar and pestle that a Richmond druggist had given to her. A bit of yellow cornmeal for flavor, water, salt, sugar and a little sorghum or maple molasses were added and the mix was cooked.

Mention of Mammy Lou's wonderful spoon bread was occasionally found in the newspapers long after she had purchased her freedom and that of her children and moved to Lexington.

FRENCH TIPTON AND HIS PAPERS

Robert Grise

A lot of people interested in Madison County history and in tracing genealogy back to pioneer days have heard of the French Tipton Papers preserved in the Special Collections and Archives at the EKU Crabbe Library. Tipton's loose papers, ancient original documents, photos and handwritten notebooks have been one of the major sources of information for just about every publication dealing with the history of Madison County. However, few seem to know of that fascinating character French Tipton.

Tipton was a tall, thin nineteenth-century Richmond man who had a stormy career as a public figure. Born near Boonesborough in 1848, French

Tipton was a graduate of Madison Male Academy and Central University and, at various times, was a non-practicing attorney, distillery gauger, teacher, world traveler, news correspondent, newspaper editor and historian.

When he was the first and only graduate of Central University in 1875, he made the valedictory address at commencement, showing his understanding of politics and cultural history. He delighted his audience with his wit and humor, as well as his knowledge.

During the remainder of his life, he was a sought-after speaker at many public functions—sometimes humorous, sometimes disturbing in plain-spoken criticisms, but always interesting.

Teaching and the law did not hold his interest for long, and he moved into the field of journalism. At various times he was the editor of all three weekly

French Tipton's (1848–1900) manuscript and collection of newspaper clippings, correspondence, photographs and other documents chronicle events in the early history of Madison County.

Richmond newspapers, the *Kentucky Register*, the *Climax* and the *Pantagraph*. As he went about getting the news, he collected a lot of old pioneer deeds, letters, photographs and bills of sale. He kept several notebooks of information on old Madison County families and events as he obtained information for obituaries and feature stories that appeared in the newspapers.

Tipton knew that no comprehensive history of Madison County had been written and that he had in his possession a collection of history data that no one else had, a detailed chronology covering the years 1770–1899. He announced that he would write a comprehensive county history but was killed in a fight in 1900 while the work was still in progress.

Tipton and Clarence E. Woods, a politically opposing editor of another Richmond newspaper, had taken rather strong "potshots" at each other editorially, and when they happened to attend the same public meetings, they frequently fell into strong verbal exchanges.

On the evening of Saturday, September 1, 1900, Woods was talking to acquaintances on Main Street when Tipton walked up to him and struck him in the left eye. Woods reeled back and then drew his pistol and shot Tipton in the abdomen. He lingered for two days until he died. Woods did not stand trial because it was decided that he was acting in self-defense. He was later elected mayor of Richmond in 1904.

During the 1930s, the late Dr. J.T. Dorris, professor of history at Eastern, obtained the French Tipton Papers, documents, photographs and notebooks, which had been piled loosely in an old trunk. He used them in writing our first comprehensive history, *Glimpses of Historic Madison County, Kentucky* (1955) and then donated them to Eastern.

PIONEERS CARSON, KINKEAD AND WOLFSKILL WENT TO NEW MEXICO

Fred Engle

Between the years 1827 and 1828, three Madison County natives saw each other and worked together in far off Taos, New Mexico. They were Christopher (Kit) Carson, Mathew Kinkead and William Wolfskill.

Carson was born on December 24, 1809, on a hill above Tates Creek (then spelled Tate's). There is a historical marker along Tates Creek Road near Carson's birthplace. Kit's father Lindsey was first married to Lucy Bradley, by whom he had five children. After Lucy died, he married Rebecca Robinson, who bore him six children in Kentucky, Christopher Houston being the sixth. Thus there were thirteen persons in the Tates Creek log cabin of three rooms and a loft. The children slept in the loft. When Kit was about 1½, the Carsons moved west to Missouri. Soon after his sixteenth birthday, Kit ran away from home, following a wagon train that ended up in Taos.

Carson's first job in Taos's was working for Mathew Kinkead, who was born in Madison County back in 1795 and had also lived in the Boonslick area of Missouri, where Kit grew up. Kinkead was famous in his own right—an early Santa Fe trader, one of Taos's first distillers, Colorado's first cattleman and a founder of Fort Pueblo. His father, David Kinkead, had built Fort Kinkead in Missouri. And although Kinkead opened his home in Taos to the fellow Madison Countian, Kit never seemed to like or speak well of him.

That same year (1827–28), William Wolfskill and Ewing Young opened a store to outfit trappers for the mountains in the booming (population 3,606) town of Taos. Carson worked at the store that winter. Wolfskill was born in Madison County on March 20, 1798. He moved on to Missouri, too, before joining William Pope in blazing the Spanish Trail from Santa Fe to Los Angeles. Wolfskill is known as the father of the California citrus fruit industry, having been one of the first to introduce this commercial venture on the West Coast.

Carson later became the most well known of the three for his adventures in the western frontier as a scout for the army officer and explorer John C. Fremont. Carson was a frontiersman and trapper who married

The exploits of adventurer and Madison County native Christopher (Kit) Carson (1809–1868) became the subject of many novels and frontier stories as his fame grew. Carson City, Nevada, is named after him.

three times. He was involved in the Mexican-American War, the Civil War and is also known for his involvement with Native Americans and military campaigns in the western states.

Thus, three Madison Countians met in Taos, the crossroads of the West, over 180 years ago.

JAMES MCCREARY: SOLDIER, STATESMAN, PATRIOT

Fred Engle

James Bennett McCreary was twice elected Governor of Kentucky, one of the few men so honored. Since the Civil War, only A.B. (Happy) Chandler, Paul Patton and Steve Beshear have also achieved this feat. Chandler waited twenty years, (1935 & 1955) while McCreary went thirty-six years between elections (1875 & 1911). Patton and Beshear were reelected after the 1992 Kentucky constitutional amendment allowed the governor of Kentucky to serve consecutive terms.

McCreary was born in Madison County on July 8, 1838, the son of Dr. Edmund and Sabrina McCreary. He graduated from Centre College and received a law degree from Cumberland University in Tennessee. He practiced law in Richmond from 1859 until August of 1862, when he joined the Eleventh Kentucky Cavalry, Confederate States of America. This local area fighting group was organized as a result of the Confederate victory at the Battle of Richmond and was commanded by Colonel David Walker Chenault of Foxtown.

Upon Colonel Chenault's death in 1863, McCreary was promoted from major to lieutenant colonel. He commanded a regiment under John Hunt Morgan of Lexington and was captured during the Ohio Raid. Imprisoned with many others from that raid, Morgan managed to escape from the stockade in Columbus, Ohio, but McCreary remained a prisoner. Offered a parole, McCreary refused to swear allegiance to the Union and was kept in prison. Finally he was exchanged for Union officers kept in Confederate prisons and rejoined the battle with General John C. Breckinridge in Virginia.

After the war McCreary married Katherine Hughes of Fayette County and they had a son, Robert. The McCreary home is still standing at 527 West Main Street in Richmond.

Entering politics, the war veteran was state representative from 1869 to 1875 (Speaker of the House for two terms) before his first election as governor (1875). From 1885 to 1897, he was a U.S. Congressman and, from 1903 to 1909, a U.S. Senator. The Federal Building on West Main Street in Richmond was built during McCreary's term as Senator. It now serves as the Madison Hall of Justice and was previously the post office, a federal court building and city hall. Returning from Washington, McCreary was again elected governor (1911).

James B. McCreary died on October 8, 1918 and was buried in the Richmond Cemetery. Two stones mark his grave: a family marker and a boulder with a bronze plaque erected by the state in 1958. Fittingly, the then Governor Chandler was the speaker at the unveiling.

Cassius M. Clay's Fight at Foxtown

Fred Engle

Much has been written about Cassius Marcellus Clay, the well-known emancipationist, nicknamed the "Lion of White Hall." His elaborate family home, originally called Clermont, was built by his father. It was renamed White Hall when Cassius and his wife made additions to the house in the 1860s. White Hall is one of the finest structures in the county and is on the National Register of Historic Places. It is a state shrine, houses a museum and is open for public tours.

Clay was born at the Clermont estate near Richmond to General Green Clay and Sally Lewis Clay on October 19, 1810, a wealthy slaveholding household. The anti-slavery stance Clay developed helped him became a leader in the county and nation as a politician, anti-slavery newspaper publisher, military leader and minister to Russia under President Lincoln. He helped start Berea College and was a cousin to noted politician Henry Clay. His daughters Mary Barr Clay and Laura Clay became political leaders in their own right, becoming leaders in the women's suffrage movement.

The "Lion of White Hall" had many duels and confrontations during his life as a public figure and was known for his skill with a bowie knife. He survived an assassination attempt in 1843 at a political debate. He fought off his attacker, Sam Brown, after being shot in the chest. As Clay continued his anti-slavery crusade, he met heated opposition, including an altercation with members of the Turner family.

In 1849, Kentucky was electing members of a constitutional convention to revise the state constitution. Slavery was a big issue. On Friday, June 15,

Cassius M. Clay (1810–1903) was a Republican, abolitionist, veteran of both the Mexican War and Civil War, and wrote a book on fighting with the Bowie knife—and was experienced in its use. Clay was one of Madison County's most interesting and eccentric characters. He died on July 22, 1903, at the age of ninety-three, and was buried in the Richmond Cemetery.

of that year a regimental muster was taking place in Foxtown in Madison County. The area was near the Lexington-Richmond Turnpike (U.S. 25) and is now known more often as the White Hall community. Squire Turner, the pro-slavery candidate for the convention from Madison County, was to address the group that afternoon, with Cassius Clay to speak in rebuttal.

Turner ripped into Clay with a violent denunciation, claiming he was at fault for the recent stampede of slaves in Fayette County. When Clay took the stand and began to reply in kind, Cyrus Turner, the candidate's eldest son, rushed at him calling him a liar and striking him a blow in the face. As the Turner crowd closed in on him, Clay drew his bowie knife, but he was struck in the head with a club by Alfred Turner, and the knife was taken from him. Thomas Turner, Cyrus's brother, stuck a revolver in Clay's face and pulled the trigger three times, but the caps failed to explode. Clay grabbed back his knife by the blade, cutting his fingers to the bone. At the same moment, he was stabbed in the left breast over the heart. Clay answered this thrust by burying his bowie knife to the hilt in the abdomen of Cyrus Turner. This is all according to the *Lexington Observer and Reporter*, editions June 16 and July 7, 1849.

A telegram was sent to Clay's mother in Frankfort, telling her he was dying. Although the paper later reported him dead, Clay did not die but recovered to fight another day. Turner, however, "expired," as the papers put it then, about midnight on Saturday, June 16. Thus ended the fight at Foxtown.

PRESTON GORDON WAS MADISON'S MASTER DRUMMER

Robert Grise

Unfortunately, a lot of Madison County persons who made significant contributions to their community in the past have long been forgotten. One of our forgotten heroes was African American drummer Preston Gordon.

Born in 1817, Preston was a slave on the farm of John Harris, about two miles from Richmond. As a small boy, he had a strong sense of rhythm and was frequently found beating on pots, pans, kettles, barrels or anything else that would make a sound. Later in life, Preston would recall that his old master would "cane him" if he left some dents in tin ware.

Preston Gordon obtained a real drum in 1829 and was hired to beat out the rhythm for company musters of militia organized at Foxtown under the direction of Captain Napoleon Tevis. After about five or six years, he became the drummer for battalion musters under Colonels Dan White and John Miller. As his reputation spread, he also was employed as a drummer for militia companies in Garrard and Lincoln Counties. Colonel William Harris's Thirty-Fifth Regiment, which was formed east of Richmond, also had Gordon as their drummer.

During the Mexican War, our Madison County drummer saw frequent service under General Cassius M. Clay and Captain James Stone. About this time, Gordon acquired a very fine drum, which had been made here in Madison County, and it was his prized possession for the rest of his life.

In addition to military events, Gordon's artistic cadence and stirring "roles and ruffles" entertained the crowds at Fourth of July celebrations and masonic ceremonies. He drummed up excitement at the laying of the cornerstones of the Methodist Episcopal Church, at the corner of Second and Irvine Streets, in 1841. He also drummed cadence at the cornerstone ceremonies of other buildings, including the Madison Female Institute.

Preston Gordon's greatest day was when he drummed the beat for 5,000 soldiers and a lot of national and local political leaders marching from the Phoenix Hotel to the Lexington Cemetery for the ceremonies for the erection of that great monument honoring the late Senator Henry Clay, who might well have become president if politics had been different. After arriving, Preston Gordon was stationed at the cemetery gates to beat out cadence for the entire long procession as it entered the cemetery. Later, he said, "I hit that little drum until I got so hot I got cold."

In 1864, Gordon joined the U.S. Army and was soon drum major for the all-black 114th Kentucky Infantry. While his outfit was with the Army of the Potomac, Gordon won first place in a contest of over 100 drum majors, and he received a gold-headed baton. When he retired a couple of years later, the soldiers took up a collection and bought him an expensive, high-quality drum.

Significant persons in our past like Preston Gordon, who had a life of service doing what he loved to do, should not ever be lost from our history.

LAURA CLAY AND BELLE BENNETT

Fred Engle

Miss Laura Clay, the daughter of Cassius M. Clay and Mary Jane Warfield Clay, was born on February 9, 1849, at the White Hall mansion. She went to Russia with her parents in 1861. She attended the University of Michigan and State College in Lexington, a rare thing for a woman in that day.

In 1888, she became president of the Kentucky Equal Rights Association and held that position for twenty-four years. She helped open Central University and organized a School of Pharmacy for Women. She opposed drinking liquor and was active in the Woman's Christian Temperance Union (WCTU).

She was a states righter, favoring individual states making decisions rather than the federal government, and broke with the Equal Rights Association in 1918 because they favored a federal constitutional amendment granting women the right to vote. She formed her own organization in 1920, which became the League of Women Voters. Unlike her father, she was a Democrat. At the 1920 National Democratic Convention, she was nominated for the presidency, the first woman to have been nominated at a major party convention for our country's highest position. In 1923 she ran for state senator but lost to the Republican opponent. Miss Clay died in Lexington on June 29, 1941, at age ninety-two and was buried in the Lexington Cemetery.

Also important to the history of women's rights in Madison County was a visit by national civil rights leader Susan B. Anthony. In 1879, Anthony came to the Richmond home of Mrs. Mary Barr Clay, Laura's older sister, to help form the Madison County Equal Rights Association. Besides Mrs. Clay, charter members were Mrs. Rollins Burnam, Mrs. Mary Ann Collins, Mrs. Lester Sommers, Mrs. E.E. McCann and Mrs. Martha Haley.

Madison County has a rich history of activism and leadership during the women's suffrage movement. In 1917, the Madison County Equal Rights Association planted a "suffrage" potato patch behind Blair Park in Richmond, helping to provide food for the war effort.

Isabel (Belle) Harris Bennett was born on December 3, 1852, six miles from Richmond on Lexington Pike (U.S. 25). On both sides of her family she was descended from early Virginia settlers and the pioneers of Fort Boonesborough. Early in life she became involved in the Methodist Episcopal Church, South. She rose to international reputation as a great organizer, fundraiser and powerful platform speaker in the area of education. For many years, she was one of the few top representatives of her church (as highly respected as bishops) to many national and international meetings, including international missionary conventions in Edinburgh in 1910 and Panama in 1916. She was the only female member of the joint commission, which planned the centennial celebration of Methodist missions work in the U.S.

In 1896, after touring eastern Kentucky and seeing the need for improved education, she established a college in London for the advanced education of public school teachers. She named it in honor of her deceased sister, Sue Bennett. She also helped establish Scarritt Bible and Training School originally in Kansas City, Missouri, and the Methodist-related Bennett

College in Rio de Janeiro, Brazil, was named in her honor. Bennett was also involved in bringing together several women's missionary groups to establish a health center and school of nursing in Shanghai, China.

In 1910, Bennett became president of the Women's Missionary Council of the Southern Methodist Church. She helped establish the Madison County Colored Chautauqua in 1915 and brought George Washington Carver and William E.B. DuBois to Richmond. In 1916, she received a Doctor of Laws degree from Kentucky Wesleyan College. She lived in the Bennett House on West Main Street in Richmond, now a bed and breakfast. Miss Bennett died July 21, 1922 and was buried in the Richmond Cemetery.

THREE AFRICAN AMERICAN LEADERS

Robert Grise

Among the many early African American leaders of Madison County after the Civil War were Reverend Harry Dunson, Reverend Madison Campbell and Henry Allen Laine.

Harry Dunson (1816-1893) was the son of slaves of the Tunstall and later the Dunson families. Because of his diligent work and honesty, he was allowed to obtain enough education that he could study on his own. He became an avid reader of books, especially the Bible, in which he had great interest. In 1842, when he was twenty-six years old, he was licensed to preach by the all-white Red Lick Baptist Church. After that time, he was known as Elder Dunson.

On December 2, 1867, Elder Dunson became the pastor of Goodloe Baptist Church near Brassfield, which had been built the previous year. He served this church twenty-six years until his death. It was said the church served a large area in Madison and adjacent counties and that it flourished without dissension under his leadership. Dunson was so respected and admired that his funeral service was attended by a large crowd of people of both races.

The Reverend Madison Campbell (1823–1897) was a widely known and highly respected Baptist preacher. From 1858 to 1896, he served as pastor of the United Colored Baptist Church, now named First Baptist Church, on the corner of Francis and Collins Streets in Richmond. The congregation has had many pastors who were outstanding leaders in improving the community.

Henry Allen Laine (1870–1955) was a Madison County teacher and a published poet of considerable reputation in the first half of the twentieth

Madison Campbell (1823–1897) preached at a number of county churches, including New Liberty, Mt. Pleasant, Otter Creek, Mt. Nebo, Goodloe Chapel and Kirksville, in addition to serving the congregation of the United Colored Baptist Church in Richmond for nearly forty years.

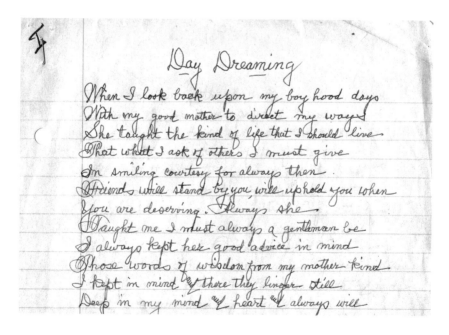

African American poet Henry Allen Laine (1870–1955) remembers his mother's good advice in this stanza of one of his many manuscripts, found in the EKU Library Special Collections and Archives.

century. He learned hard work as a youth and attended Berea College. He taught school in Madison County for twenty-one years and was chairman of the county Colored Teachers Association for twenty of those years.

Laine invested himself freely in the lives of countless children over the years and was highly respected as a leader. He may be best known now for his poetry, especially his book of poems *Footprints*, which was so popular that it was reprinted several times.

Laine was frequently asked to read his poetry at the state Kentucky Negro Education Association and at schools and churches. A line in one of his poems is still occasionally quoted: "These three things complete the man: love, refinement, and the dollar."

THE STORY OF THE HERMIT OF COLLEGE HILL

Fred Engle

In 1988, Faye Click sent me the following story, which Molly Wagers Durbin wrote for Mrs. Click's Kentucky history class at the Waco School where she taught.

Mrs. Click said that the man lived on land owned by her father, S.F. Winkler on Holiday Lane off of College Hill Road. Winkler's farm was a part of the old Hisle farm. When the Winklers moved to the farm in 1936, they were told of the hermit. Some of the rock walls of his house were still standing. It was told that the hermit did odd jobs for the Hisles and that he especially liked to chop wood.

Here then is the story of the hermit of College Hill, as told by Molly Durbin. It all took place in the early part of the twentieth century.

THE HERMIT OF COLLEGE HILL

The story of the hermit is true. The story was related to me by my great-aunt, Mrs. Edith Steward. Now I am going to tell you the story as it was told to me.

There was a strange hermit on the Walter Hisle farm. He let his hair and beard grow. He only had one set of clothes, and he lived in a hole in the ground with a wall built around it. It was said that he had a makeshift stove with a pipe sticking out the top to keep him warm. He lived on the game and berries he had and the food the friendly neighbors brought him.

One day my great-grandfather, Mr. Charles Searcy, wrote a story to a newspaper in Chicago, describing this hermit. Somehow, in which no one has been able to find out, this article reached a man in the northernmost part of Maine. This man wrote back to my great-grandfather that he thought this hermit was his long lost brother and asked my great grandfather to send a letter to him further describing the hermit.

When my great-grandfather wrote back, he told the color of the hermit's eyes and so on. The man wrote back telling he was sure the old hermit was his brother. He also said that while feeding cattle, his brother fell off the sled and injured his head. He was never the same after that. His brother, the hermit, had wandered away from home and was never heard from again. When his family searched and couldn't find him, they gave up, brokenhearted.

In about one month, the man from Maine arrived at Waco and asked my great-grandfather to take him to his brother. Several people had heard about this man from Maine, so when my great-grandfather took him to see the hermit, quite a few people were there.

There was such a happy reunion between the two men! Later that day, my great-grandmother had a big country supper for the two men and some of their friends. Very early the next morning the two brothers left for home and were never heard from again.

VETERANS' STORIES FROM WORLD WAR II

Fred Engle

Many Madison County residents over the years have served their country with bravery and honor during national conflicts, from the Revolutionary War to the present. During World War II, many Madison County men, women and families sacrificed for the war effort. The experiences of two local men in particular make especially thrilling war-time tales. Each involves having to jump out of a plane on the other side of the world.

Bobby Jennings mainly worked on the ground to keep B-29s and other Air Corps planes flying. Once he was on a B-29, when over North Burma, near Tibet, the plane caught fire and the crew had to bail out. Bobby and others landed in a lake at the foothills of the Himalayas. Some of them drowned. Bobby was lucky and landed near a boat. The native in the boat had never seen a white man before, but he took Bobby to a nearby island. Others in the crew ended up there, too. A few days later the natives took the airmen to the last outpost of the British where they began the long trip back home.

Across the world in Northern Italy, James H. (Junior) Jackson was flying bombing missions into Austria, attacking Vienna and Innsbruck, occupied by the Nazi troops. On one mission, his plane was shot down on December 29, 1944, and he and his crew parachuted into Yugoslavia. Junior and one crewmember landed near each other on a mountaintop. They began working their way down the mountainside but at the first village found the Germans waiting—they had been spotted floating to earth and were reported.

As a prisoner of war, Junior was moved around a lot, finally ending up in "Stalag Luft l" in Barth, Germany. It was not fun like *Hogan's Heroes*. Word was sent back to the Jackson family that he was missing in action and assumed dead. Months later, when liberated by the Russians and released from the POW camp, Junior was finally able to call home across the Atlantic.

I am sure there are many exciting war tales Madison County veterans could tell. These are but two of them.

EDUCATION

MADISON ACADEMY

Robert Grise

Madison Academy, also known as Madison Seminary and Madison Male Seminary, was one of the first schools of its type that was chartered by the Kentucky Legislature. An academy was a type of secondary school started by Benjamin Franklin for the purpose of giving additional or "secondary" education to boys (only) who had completed the elementary level of training. Its curriculum contained both "college prep" courses and also practical courses such as bookkeeping for those boys not going on to college.

An act of the Kentucky General Assembly on December 22, 1798, incorporated academies in each county of the state (others were encouraged), and 6,000 acres of unimproved public lands situated on the south side of the Green and Cumberland Rivers were given as an endowment for each school. The lands could be leased but not sold at that time, but later the law was changed and Madison Academy disposed of its land holdings. Also authorized was the raising of funds up to $1,000 by lottery and by subscription.

The first trustees appointed by the original charter consisted of twelve men, several of whom, including Green Clay, Joseph Kennedy and Christopher Irvine, were well known and respected. However, they apparently failed to act upon the charter, and the school was not established. In 1805, another set of five trustees was named, consisting of Robert Rodes, Archibald Woods, William Irvine, John Patrick and James Barnett. In 1816 the trustees acquired

1.5 acres on North Second Street in Richmond (across from the Regular Baptist Church) from Robert Caldwell, also one of the first trustees, for one dollar on the condition that the land be used only for educational purposes.

Tuition, which was charged for all students, varied to some extent according to the type of course for which the boy was enrolled. The usual charge at first was about five pounds English money and later about ten to fifteen dollars. County produce at market price was usually accepted in lieu of cash.

Courses of study included those commonly taught in such schools—composition, elocution, moral philosophy, Greek, Latin, history, logic, geography, astronomy, natural philosophy (natural sciences) and others such as the practical courses in bookkeeping and rapid calculation. Lecture was the standard teaching method, and prizes and other rewards were offered to improve recitation. Enrollment was small, probably less than a hundred students for much of the history of the institution.

Enrollment in the school declined and financial difficulties increased as the high school movement grew rapidly after the Civil War. In 1890, the school was transferred to the Richmond public school trustees—and that was the end of Madison Academy.

EARLY PRIVATE SCHOOLS: TEXAS SEMINARY, ELLIOTT INSTITUTE AND THE KINGSTON SCHOOL

Robert Grise

Before there was a well-established countywide public school system in Madison County, a number of private schools were established by families concerned with the education of their children. While most of them had an elementary department, they mainly existed for the purpose of preparing boys or girls who had finished the elementary level to enter college or university education.

Several small, rather exclusive private schools were started in the Foxtown area beginning about 1845 or 1850. Those Foxtown parents usually asked a college to send a young man of high moral character to teach for the school year, which was about ten months. Pay was around $75 a month, plus food and lodging in nearby homes. Another private school, Silver Creek Academy, was located in Peytontown and existed roughly from 1844 to 1871.

Among the larger private schools was Texas Seminary, which was established in the late 1860s at the village now known as College Hill. For

In Madison County's pioneer days, scholars conducted private "subscription" schools at stations or inns, or in crude log-pen schoolhouses built by local people in those neighborhoods on creeks and along the Wilderness Road system. Occasionally, the parlor of a large home was also used as a schoolroom in the early 1800s. After the period of log schoolhouses came the time of the one-room school built of rough lumber from local sawmills.

many years the school was operated by the Methodist Episcopal Church, which sent well-qualified teachers. In the 1880s, the institution became part of the county public school system.

One private academy of excellent reputation was Elliott Institute at Kirksville. It flourished from the 1870s until the early 1900s, when it was incorporated into the Kirksville public school system. Milton Elliott had taught in his own private school for some years before it was officially chartered by the state legislature in March 1882. The school had primary, preparatory (for college) and collegiate departments.

Elliot was the president of the newly chartered school and had the power to appoint such teachers "as may be necessary to instruct the pupils of said institute in the arts and sciences, and in all useful and ornamental branches of a liberal and thorough education." The charter specifically gave Elliott the power to "remove same at will." The president had full power to prescribe and regulate the course of study and, with the advice and consent of the trustees, to manage the business affairs of the school. He also was given the power to grant diplomas to students who had completed one of the courses of study in the Institute, who had passed regular examinations in the subjects studied and who had "sustained a good moral character." One surprising section in the Elliott Institute's charter stated that the president of this small academy in Kirksville could "also confer any of the degrees and honors upon such persons as he may see fit that are now authorized by law to be conferred by any of the universities or college of this State."

In 1885, the members of the Kingston Masonic Lodge 315 discussed the lack of available education for children in their part of the county. They decided to build a combination lodge hall and schoolhouse on a one-acre lot just a little north of the main intersection at Kingston.

On February 9, 1886, the state legislature chartered the Kingston School Joint Stock Company. Shares were $10, and the charter provided for the Masonic Lodge to hold ninety-five shares as the controlling interest. The charter required that a three-member board of trustees be elected by the stockholders, with two of the three being members of the lodge.

The lodge met upstairs on the second floor and the school occupied the first. When school was not in session, the trustees could rent out the main floor for other activities such as religious "protracted meetings," political speeches or singing schools. The bylaws stated that "no spirituous, vinous or malt liquors should be sold upon any property held or owned by said company."

Education in grades 1–12 was provided as needed, at a tuition fee of about $2 per month. The school gained a good reputation, and soon students came from other parts of the county and even adjoining counties.

By 1900, free public education in grades 1–8 began to be more common as more one-room public schools were built, and the Kingston School began to operate mostly on the secondary level. Soon after 1903, the school ceased to operate altogether, for public high school education had become more readily available, and the tuition-charging private schools were not able to compete with them.

Education

RICHMOND SCHOOLS FOR GIRLS

Robert Grise and Fred Engle

There were several schools for girls established in Richmond during the first half of the nineteenth century, including the Richmond Female Academy (incorporated in 1835) and the Richmond Female Institute (incorporated in 1845).

When it opened, the trustees of the Richmond Female Academy advertised in the local weekly newspaper, the *Farmer's Chronicle*, that parents were invited to enroll their girls in this school operated by refined persons. Pupils could study music, French, painting and natural science, in addition to the basic subjects of a common English education. The teachers would not forget, the ad stated, "that a lady's influence may be greatly increased by easy and graceful manners, and by an exhibition of that refinement which results from devoting some attention to Music, Painting, Poetry, etc."

The tuition for the preparatory department for the 1842–43 five-month school year was $8 to $15, depending on which studies were selected. For "higher education," which was on the level of our high school, not college, the fee was $18. French and Latin (which all refined young ladies were expected to be acquainted with) cost an additional $15, as did instruction in painting and drawing. Twenty-five boarders could be accommodated in the house of the teachers, the school's 1842 *Farmer's Chronicle* ad stated. Girls who did not have another definite choice of church to attend on Sunday morning would be taken by their teachers to the Presbyterian Church services.

A later school for girls was the Madison Female Institute, also known as the Madison Female School or Academy. It was organized around 1853 by leaders of the First Christian Church of Richmond for the education of young ladies. That year, they purchased the brick residence of Major McClanahan, situated on a hill overlooking the city.

The school opened its doors under the principalship of W.B. Smith and, in 1858, trustees were named and the Madison Female School was chartered by the state. Located on the top of the hill now occupied by Madison Middle School, the school's reputation grew as it attracted many students.

Students from several parts of Kentucky and other states attended the Institute. The school was listed among the famous southern finishing schools for girls. The school had three parts—primary, intermediate and collegiate (really college preparatory).

55

The grounds consisted of ten acres, divided into lawns, tennis courts and gardens. It was close to town, yet rural in atmosphere. The buildings were large and commodious. The house had hot and cold water, bathrooms, closets, electric lights and hot water heat. To quote the old school authorities, "Everything womanly is encouraged and emphasized, and everything that is loud, masculine and pedantic is discouraged."

Pupils were chaperoned to and from the churches of their parents' choice, as well as shopping, calling, to and from trains and to and from all entertainments. Graduates of the collegiate department were prepared and qualified to enter the large Eastern colleges.

To quote a 1910 issue of the *Richmond Climax*, "We honestly believe that no educational institution throughout the length and breadth of the country is better qualified to train the minds and bodies of our girls into

Altogether, there were about 300 graduates from the Madison Female Institute, the girls' finishing school located on the top of the hill where Madison Middle School now stands in Richmond. This photo shows the 1914 graduating class. The school existed from 1853 to 1919, and offered a wide range of curriculum.

the paths that lead to usefulness and respect and to the up-building of noble women."

In 1862, during the Battle of Richmond, the school was used as a hospital for wounded soldiers. In 1863, the trustees of the school filed a claim against the government for damage to the school. Fifty-two years later, in May of 1915, they were paid $5,200. In 1890, Mrs. Alexander Campbell, wife of one of the founders of the Disciples of Christ, spent time at the school. Alice Lloyd, who would later found Alice Lloyd College in Pippa Passes, Kentucky, served as principal of the school for a time.

Because of increased availability of free public education, schools like Madison Female Institute suffered declining enrollments in the early 1900s. In 1919, the school was permanently closed and its property leased to the Richmond Board of Education for ninety-nine years.

THE FOUNDING OF BEREA

Fred Engle

In 1853, abolitionist John G. Fee, under the sponsorship of Cassius M. Clay, organized an anti-slavery church in the old Glades Church House in the southern part of Madison County. From this grew the city of Berea and Berea College. It was called by the Bible name, Berea, because the people "received the Word with all readiness of mind," as quoted in Acts 17:11.

A schoolhouse was built in the area in 1855, and a board of trustees was formed in 1858. Berea College adopted a constitution and bylaws in 1859. The anti-slavery position of the school faculty and administration upset the local citizens. In 1859, a large county convention was held in Richmond to discuss the Berea College "problem." A committee of sixty-five prominent county citizens was appointed and, on December 23, 1859, this committee notified the faculty at Berea that they had ten days to leave the state.

The faculty appealed to the governor for protection, but he said he could not guarantee their safety. So the faculty and their families (around forty in all) left for Cincinnati and points north. After the Civil War, in 1865, the board of trustees was reorganized, a charter obtained and the school was soon after reopened.

In 1869, college-level classes began. Before that, classes were college preparatory, with primary, intermediate, preparatory, normal and ladies' departments. Hence in 1873, the first A.B. degrees were granted. The

With a history of promoting interracial and coeducational opportunities for students, Berea College has been a leader in the county and the nation. The school has also focused on Appalachia as its primary service region. Berea has been known for the unique handicrafts produced by its students. This photo from 1926 shows students weaving on hand looms.

unincorporated village became a formal city in 1890 via an act passed by the General Assembly. In 1896, John L. Gay was appointed clerk of the Board of Trustees. He later served forty years as mayor of Berea.

In 1904, the Day Law was passed in Kentucky prohibiting the mixing of races in schools, targeting Berea, the only interracial school in the state. The Day Law was upheld by the Supreme Court in 1908, forcing Berea to segregate. Berea College then assisted in the establishment of Lincoln Institute, a school for black students near Shelbyville. The law changed again in 1950, and interracial classes returned to the college.

Through the years Berea College has stayed true to its motto "God has made of one blood all peoples of the earth."

BEREA COLLEGE'S LEADERS

Fred Engle

Most of us associate John G. Fee and Cassius M. Clay with the founding of Berea and Berea College, but J.A.R. Rogers is not as well known. Fee was a preacher and a graduate of Lane Theological Seminary of Cincinnati (1842). He did not want to be tied down to denominational rules and regulations so he formed an independent church in Lewis County. He also published a booklet, *Antislavery Manual*, in 1848. This brought him to the attention of Cassius Clay.

Clay invited Fee to come to Madison County in 1853 and preach a series of sermons in the south end of the county. Clay liked what he heard and gave Fee a ten-acre lot for a home and church. Berea's Union Church traces its history to this early antislavery church, which consisted of 13 members. Many years later, Fee decided that the Bible only taught baptism by immersion. When the Union Church refused to adopt that doctrine, he withdrew and helped in the founding of another church, Berea Christian.

A one-room school was built in 1855 on a lot given by William B. Wright. Teachers were brought in from Oberlin College, an abolition stronghold in Ohio. In 1856, Fee's firebrand politics were too much for Clay and the two men split at a Fourth of July rally.

It was in 1858 that J.A.R. Rogers, an Oberlin graduate, came to Berea and he and his wife became the chief teachers with up to a hundred students. In 1859, Rogers, Fee and others drew up an organizational constitution for a college and arranged to buy 110 acres nearby for $1,750.

Before Berea could be fully developed, Rogers, Fee and others were driven from the community by Southern sympathizers. They returned in April 1865 with $10,000, and a legal charter was

J.A.R. Rogers and his wife Elizabeth Embree Rogers were influential early leaders at Berea College. The Rogers Art Building, completed in 1935, and the Elizabeth Embree Rogers Hall, completed in 1925, honor the couple's contributions to the institution.

secured. The school was first called the Berea Literary Institute and had 187 students and was almost evenly divided between blacks and whites.

E. Henry Fairchild, also from Oberlin, became the first president in the spring of 1869 and the first college class began in September of that year. Berea was helped a great deal during these early days by the American Missionary Association.

Fairchild served as president from 1869 to 1889. He was followed by William B. Stewart (1890–92), then William G. Frost (1892–1920). President Frost was the developer of Berea's unique Labor Program, in which students work for the college to pay for their education. He also promoted Berea's service work in the Appalachian region. Dr. William J. Hutchins was president from 1920 to 1939 and was succeeded by his son Francis S. Hutchins (1939-67). The other Berea College presidents have been Willis D. Weatherford (1968–84), John B. Stephenson (1984–94) and Larry D. Shinn (1994–present).

CENTRAL UNIVERSITY OPENED PATH FOR EKU

Robert Grise

Central University, the Southern Presbyterian institution of higher education that existed in Richmond from 1874 to 1901, was established on the site now occupied by Eastern Kentucky University. Soon after the Civil War, Southern Presbyterians were more or less excluded from control of Centre College in Danville, so they decided to establish their own institution.

Richmond finally gained the location of the new Central University, competing with Anchorage, Bardstown, Danville and Paris. After being incorporated on March 3, 1873, the institution got off to a good start in September the following year, but it was plagued by low enrollment and several financial recessions, which made it very difficult to collect pledges and raise endowment.

The College of Philosophy, Letters and Science opened in Central's University Building in the fall of 1874. It was a college for men who were to enter mainly the professions of Christian ministry, teaching, medicine, law and business management. The curriculum was pure "headbone education" in the classical liberal arts tradition—no vocational courses or such "hands on" studies as mechanics or agriculture.

The Reverend J.W. Pratt was the first president of the college in Richmond, succeeded by J.V. Logan. The Reverend Robert L. Breck, for

This circa 1894 photo shows the Central University mandolin club. Various student organizations existed at the school, including fraternities and athletics.

whose family Breck Avenue was named, was the first chancellor of the entire university; he was succeeded by the Reverend L.H. Blanton, under whose leadership the institution successfully weathered financial crisis, faculty resignations and declining enrollment. Central also had colleges of medicine, dentistry and law. In the 1890s, the College of Philosophy, Letters and Science started admitting women, probably more out of the desperate need for money and higher enrollment than out of concern for educational equality between the sexes.

Since secondary schools such as academies and high schools were somewhat scarce outside of urban centers in the state over a century ago, the university had its own college preparatory schools to prepare boys who finished the eighth grade (frequently in a one-room rural school) to enter the university. Central's own local academy was housed in a small brick building, near what is now the front of the Keen Johnson Building.

Other Central University preparatory schools were S.P. Lees Collegiate Institute at Jackson, with J.M. Moore, as president; Hardin Collegiate

Institute at Elizabethtown with Rice Miller as president; and Middlesborough University School at Middlesborough, with J.R. Sterrett, serving as president.

Central University battled financial difficulties over the years. Things became so bad in the 1879–80 school year that several faculty members left and discussions were held to consider closing its doors for good. The Southern Presbyterian school finally gave up in 1901 and turned over most of its resources, but not the campus, to Centre College. Between 1901, when Central University closed and 1906, when Eastern Kentucky State Normal School was established on the campus, Walters Collegiate Institute operated on the site as a secondary school.

A BRIEF HISTORY OF THE MODEL SCHOOL

Fred Engle

The Model School, later known as the Training School and still later as Model Laboratory School, opened September 11, 1906, four months before classes began at Eastern Kentucky State Normal School. It was, in a sense, a continuation of the Walters Collegiate Institute.

The twelve grades were operated from that date until 1922, when under pressure from the state superintendent and the Richmond city superintendent, the high school division was shut down. A junior high was opened in 1925 and, in 1930, Model High School opened for business again after an eight-year layoff. From 1927 to 1930, a Normal High School operated on Eastern's campus during the transition of the Normal School into a State Teachers College.

Model first occupied the old Central University building and then moved to the Roark Building. In 1918, the school moved into the Cammack Building and, with the reinstitution of the high school in 1930, Model occupied both Cammack (Elementary) and University (Junior High-High School).

During its early years, Model had a cadet corps and participated in interscholastic sports, such as football, baseball, track and basketball. A rural school network was operated within the Model system from 1918 until about 1958. One operated on the college campus; another, Kavanaugh, on the Irvine Pike; a third, Green's Chapel on Barnes Mill; and the last on the Lancaster Pike, where the new Model building was later opened in 1961.

The building along Lancaster Avenue was named after Herman L. Donovan, Eastern's fourth president. The auditorium was named in honor

The Model School, which has always been affiliated with Eastern, dates back to 1906. The building locations and the school's mascot have changed over the years, but Model continues to provide excellent education to children from preschool through the twelfth grade. This photo from the 1960s features the Model High School "Rebels" marching band.

of R.A. Edwards, who served as director of the Training School, and the library was named in honor of May C. Hansen, faculty member at the Training School for forty years.

Model also participated in a joint scholastic and athletic program with Madison High from 1939 to 1961. Known as Madison-Model High School, students took classes at both places, played ball together and even participated in joint graduation ceremonies.

For many years, Model had both a director and a high school principal. Serving as director during this time were Colonel Edgar Hesketh Crawford (1907–1908), Ira Waite Jayne (1908–1909), E. George Payne (1909–1910), who held a PhD from the University of Bonn, Germany, President J.G. Crabbe of the Normal School (1910–1916), President T.J. Coates of the Normal School (1916–1918), Richard A. Edwards (1918–1954), M.E. Mattox (acting, 1924–1925). Upon Mr. Edwards's retirement in 1954, Dr. J.D. Coates became director. From 1961 until the present, Model has had only a director.

Some Significant Dates in Eastern's History

Fred Engle

For newcomers to the community and for those with short memories, here are some significant dates in the history of Eastern Kentucky University.

In 1874, Central University of Richmond, a Southern Presbyterian school, was founded. Two buildings still standing on Eastern's campus date back to Central University. The Blanton House was built in 1886 and is named for Central's last chancellor, Lindsey Hughes Blanton (1832–1914). Two years after Central closed in 1901, the house was sold to Lucy Gibbs Patton for $6,050. The next owner was Thompson S. Burnam. In 1912, he sold it to the Normal School for $12,500. It became the president's house and has remained such until this day.

The other old building from the Presbyterian days is the University Building, which was built in 1874. Designed by architect Cincinnatus Shryock, it has three stories and a full basement. It cost $30,000, and the brick was produced at a kiln nearby. It technically faces Lancaster Avenue. It is on this side that you can see Central's motto in Latin: *Lex, Rex-Crux, Lux,* or "Law, King-Cross, Light." Good Presbyterian doctrine.

The University Building was the main classroom building for Central University. It then housed Walters Collegiate Institute (1901–1906) after Central University merged with Centre College of Danville in 1901, a Northern Presbyterian school. Model High was also at one time housed in the University Building. My coauthor and I attended Model's seventh through twelfth grades there. An auditorium was on the second floor. Later, while on the Eastern faculty, I occupied my old principal's office on the first floor. It is now a classroom building, partially attached to the library.

In 1906, Eastern Kentucky State Normal School was established with Ruric Nevel Roark as its first president. In 1909, Mrs. Mary C. Roark became acting president. Also in 1909, the Roark Building was built along Lancaster Avenue and was named in honor of the school's first leader.

In 1910, John Grant Crabbe became president. The library is named after him. The present library building is built around a core made of the old library. In 1916, Thomas Jackson Coates was elected president. The Normal School built the Cammack building in 1918. It was named for James W. Cammack, a member of the first Board of Regents. My coauthor and I attended the Training School there, first grade through sixth.

In 1922, Eastern became a four-year institution under the name of Eastern Kentucky State Normal School and Teachers College. The Coates Building was built in 1926. Named for the third president, it became the main administration building. My father, Dr. Fred A. Engle Sr., occupied an office on the second story of Coates for many years. The Hiram Brock auditorium in the Coates Building was dedicated in 1930.

In 1928, Herman Lee Donovan became president. I might add that my father joined the Eastern faculty that year. In 1930, the school was renamed Eastern Kentucky State Teachers College and, in 1935, a graduate program was begun leading to the Master of Arts in Education. Originally men's

This photo of the old Hanger Stadium on Eastern's campus shows the school's growth during Robert Martin's administration. In the 1960s, increases in enrollment prompted a building boom on the campus. Construction of Palmer Hall and the library addition are seen in this aerial.

dormitories, the Beckham, McCreary and Miller buildings were built by the Works Progress Administration (WPA) in 1938, and were named for politicians who helped establish Eastern in Richmond.

The Keen Johnson Building, known for many years as the student union, was constructed between 1939 and 1940 by the WPA. It was named for Richmond resident Keen Johnson (1896–1960), who was Kentucky's governor from 1939–1943. It was a show place for many years (Walnut Hall in particular is a place of beauty). Also, in 1939, Dr. Presley M. Grise, my coauthor's father, began teaching at Eastern after teaching at Model, starting in 1930. In 1941, William Francis O'Donnell was elected president. In 1948, the Kentucky General Assembly removed the word "Teachers" from the name and granted Eastern the right to award nonprofessional degrees.

In 1960, Robert R. Martin was elected president, beginning a building boom on the campus. In 1966 came another name change as the state college became Eastern Kentucky University. In 1976, J.C. Powell became the seventh president and, in 1979, an academic reorganization resulted in several new colleges. In case you are interested in some other dates, I came to Eastern's faculty in 1959, and my coauthor came in 1963.

In 1984, Hanly Funderburk became president, followed by Robert Kustra in 1998. Joanne Glasser became the university's first female president in 2001, and Charles Douglas Whitlock became Eastern's eleventh president in 2007.

1906–1910: DR. AND MRS. ROARK HEADED EASTERN

Robert Grise

When Eastern was first founded in 1906 by the Kentucky General Assembly, it was a "state normal school," a secondary-level institution for the education of teachers, who, for the most part, would teach in the hundreds of public one-room rural elementary schools in the eastern half of the state.

Western, in Bowling Green, was founded at the same time in the same legislative bill, but we sometimes tease our friends and relatives at Western, saying, "Eastern was founded first a whole paragraph ahead of Western!"

It was at the very first meeting of Eastern's Board of Regents that Dr. Ruric Nevel Roark was chosen as the first president of Eastern, so unlike the modern searches for university presidents that usually take several months.

Dr. Roark had been the popular head of the "Normal School Department" at that state college in Lexington that became the University of Kentucky in 1916. Dr. Roark seemed to be perfect for the new position. He threw himself wholeheartedly into the selection of the first faculty, the defining of goals, the raising of funds and the design of the first (of many) curriculum. In just three years, he wore himself out so completely for the school he believed in that he died of cancer in April 1909. The administration/classroom building under construction at the time was named in his honor.

The Board of Regents then did an unusual but courageous (for those days) thing. They appointed Mrs. Roark as acting president! She was a very able administrator and, had she not been a woman, she more than likely would have been chosen as the second president of Eastern.

An intelligent and educated woman in the days when it was unusual for women to go to college at all, she had attended Nebraska University, Oberlin College, National Normal University and Colorado College and had earned both AB and BS degrees. She had been a classroom teacher and then vice-president of Glasgow Normal School while her husband was president there. No wonder then that she was an effective administrator.

In October 1909, the Board of Regents appointed Mrs. Roark dean of women. She then served both in the deanship and as the acting president until John Grant Crabbe was named president in April 1910. Mrs. Roark continued in the office of dean of women until 1915.

HIRAM BROCK AUDITORIUM: A SOURCE OF PLEASANT MEMORIES

Fred Engle

Many people in Madison County have pleasant memories of Hiram Brock Auditorium on the campus of Eastern Kentucky University. College and high school graduations have been held there. Plays, musicals and movies have been performed there. Chapel, or assembly, used to be held there for all Eastern students, then just the freshmen. Now even that group is too large for the 1,700-seat auditorium.

The auditorium was dedicated on April 15, 1930 and is named for an Eastern regent from Harlan, Hiram M. Brock, who served from May 8, 1914, to April 26, 1930, and again from April 27, 1932, to January 10, 1936. Reciting the words, "We dedicate this auditorium" after each phrase, the group that gathered that day dedicated Hiram Brock Auditorium to the following:

> *The worship of God; the end that within these walls we happily may find Him whom to know aright is Life Eternal; the service of our nation, the glory of our Commonwealth, the enrichment of our smallest governmental unit; the hope that men and women assembled here may depart with the high ideal of patriotism, with the great desire for service, and with the ambition to be useful citizens; the amelioration of all classes, the improvement of all professions, but more especially to that of teaching and learning; believing as we do that ignorance is the great curse of mankind, that without learning there is no vision, and that without vision the people perish; the contemplation of beauty, the understanding of music, the inspiration of oratory; community life, college comradeship, and the spirit of friendliness; the youth of our Commonwealth who hunger and thirst for knowledge, who seek to attain scholarship that they may realize the joys that enlightenment brings as well as the opportunities for a life of greater usefulness; the memory of those who have put their lives into this institution, whose very life blood has been poured into the building of this building, whose spirit emanates from its every recess; the service of those yet among us and of those to come after whose lives*

This 1930s photo of the interior of Brock Auditorium shows the view from the stage. Brock Auditorium is housed in the Coates Administration Building on Eastern's campus.

*will be molded in similar patterns of unselfish altruism; finally, to whatsoever things
are true, to whatsoever things are honest, to whatsoever things are just, to whatsoever
things are pure, to whatsoever things are lovely, to whatsoever things are of good report.*

Another world? No, just the way people thought in 1930. I wonder how many buildings are dedicated to these things today? Regardless of changing times, Hiram Brock Auditorium is still with us and just as beautiful as it was eighty years ago, dedicated to God, education, beauty and truth.

RICHMOND CITY SCHOOLS: CALDWELL AND MADISON HIGH

Robert Grise

The Caldwell High School, with grades 1–12, was erected in 1894, on the corner of North Second Street and Moberly Avenue in Richmond, the former site of the old Madison Male Academy. It was dedicated in January

This circa 1909 postcard depicts the Caldwell High School, on the corner of North Second Street and Moberly Avenue, on the former site of the old Madison Male Academy. This public school served Richmond from 1894 to 1921.

1895 and served until it burned (set to fire by an arsonist, it was said) in 1921. Caldwell High classes were then held in church basements, rented rooms and even the city police courtroom.

At the time of World War I, there were three high schools for white students in Richmond—Caldwell High (the public school), Madison Female Institute and Model High (private schools). In 1919, the city board of education obtained a ninety-nine-year lease on the old Madison Female Institute campus "on the hill," when that well-known and respected girls' private finishing school went out of business due to the increasing availability of free public education. There was a main building made of brick and several smaller wooden structures. After renovations, Madison High School opened in 1920 in the old Female Institute buildings. Caldwell burned in 1921 and, in 1922, the high school part of Model was abolished, so Richmond went from three high schools for white students in 1919 to one (Madison High) in 1922.

Madison High School (grades 1–12) was housed in the building "on the hill" in Richmond from 1923 to 1989. This photo from the 1960s shows members of the Madison High girls' softball team wearing their "Royal Purples" sweatshirts.

In 1922, the old Female Institute buildings were torn down, and construction was started on large new two-story brick building to house Madison High. Although called Madison High School, the school was for white public school children in grades 1–12.

The official dedication of the new Madison High School building was held on June 15, 1923, with a great celebration lasting most of the afternoon. A parade of school children, led by the American Legion band, marched to the new building, followed by the members of the Board of Trustees of the Madison Female Institute, the Richmond City Council and the Richmond Board of Education.

The top floor of the Madison High School building was added shortly after the end of World War II. The building went through several other renovations over the years and was merged with Model High from 1939 to 1961, with students taking classes at both schools and participating in joint scholastic and athletic activities.

Madison High School served Richmond students until 1989, when the Richmond Independent School district consolidated with the county school system and students went to Madison Central. The Madison High building was rededicated by the Madison County Board of Education as Madison Middle School on September 22, 1992, continuing the tradition of excellent public school education in the city of Richmond.

"Richmond High Forever"

Fred Engle

An early school for African American students was held in the First Baptist Church (Francis and Collins Streets) in Richmond, and Miss Josie Foeman was the teacher. The school, known as the Richmond City (Colored) School, began in 1896. Later, Mrs. Bell Jackson was the main teacher. After completing six grades, pupils went on to Berea Academy to high school. The Richmond City School, under the leadership of Charles Reynolds, moved to a Hill Street location.

With the development of the Dillingham subdivision, a new larger building was constructed on East Main where Richmond High was located for many years. It is now the site of the Telford YMCA. A ten-room brick building featuring a tower for the school bell was built in 1900 under the leadership of principal J.D.M. Russell, and the school soon became known as Richmond High School.

Later additions were made to the building, and the school added a two-year high school. When Russell left, J.S. Hathaway succeeded him as principal. Other principals of the school included P.L. Guthrie, J.G. Fletcher and C.G. Merritt.

Four rooms were added to the back of the building and the school became a standard four-year high school in 1926. In 1928, the auditorium/ gymnasium was dedicated, made possible by funds raised by the citizens of Richmond. Between 1929 and 1930, the Richmond Shop, a manual training facility consisting of five rooms and financed by the Rosenwald Foundation, was added to the original building. Between 1933 and 1936, the Women's Literary Club and the Ladies Art Club purchased two lots to be used as a playground and football field for the school. The Women's Literary Club also added a library. In 1939, a gymnasium was constructed by the WPA.

With integration came the closing of Richmond High School. The last graduating class was in 1956. The site then became an integrated junior high school for grades 1–8 and was known as Richmond Elementary School. C.G. Merritt served as principal from 1945 until the closing of the school in 1973.

The old Richmond High building was then purchased by the Telford Community Center, an organization devoted to the improvement of the

The Richmond High School Ramblers won the 1940, 1942 and 1943 Kentucky High School Athletic League state basketball championships. The 1943 team is pictured here with Principal J.G. Fletcher in front of the Richmond High gym on East Main Street, which now houses the Telford YMCA.

Richmond community. The Telford Center had been opened in 1937 and named for Reverend Robert Lee Telford, a prominent Presbyterian pastor and outstanding Richmond citizen during the first few decades of the twentieth century. In 1986, the Telford Center became a chapter of the YMCA.

There is an active Richmond High School Alumni Association, which has annual meetings and is interested in collecting records and information concerning that school, forever a part of our history.

"Fruit Jar High"

Fred Engle

During all the years I attended Madison-Model High School (1943–47), whenever we played Berea High, our chant was "Break that fruit jar wide open." I often wondered what that battle cry against the Pirates really meant.

Various people have various explanations, but the consensus seems to run something like this: back around 1924, Berea College put into effect a rule that no one under sixteen could go to the Foundation School, which led into Berea Academy. The Foundation and Academy were a grade and high school connected with the college, much as Model is with Eastern. This was to force the establishment of a public high school in Berea.

There were two county members and three persons from the city on the Berea School Board, but no Berea High School system. Public grade school students were used to going on to the academy. The city had a small tax base because of the college land ownership, and the city board felt they could not afford a city high school. The college rule was supposed to force the city board into action.

At a Berea School Board meeting one night, out of the five-member board, only two of the three members from the city of Berea were there. They favored building a city high school, whereas the two members of the board from the county favored taking the city system into the county system. At previous meetings, they had been talking about whether the new high school should be the responsibility of the city or the county.

There was an attempt made at the meeting for the city system to join the county school system, with the two members from the county agreeing. In the middle of the argument, the secretary of the board rose, gathered the records and proceeded to leave, thus closing the meeting and stopping the move to consolidate with the county system. An irate board member grabbed a nearby fruit jar filled with flowers and threw it at the secretary, giving him a cut on the forehead.

In 1924, when Berea High was finally established under the city school system rather than the county, the citizens of the city called it "Fruit Jar High." Berea High got a new building in 1930. So when the Purples played the Pirates, we yelled, "Break that fruit jar wide open," without knowing the story of the fruit jar.

Later, the Berea Academy (the high school) changed its name, and the entire system including the high school was called Berea Foundation. Naturally, a crosstown rivalry between the city school and the college-affiliated high school grew.

One year in the 1950s, a group of Foundation supporters ran up a flag on a pole in front of Berea High. It extolled the Foundation's Lions and said bad things about the Pirates. They cut the lanyard and greased the pole. The next morning, attempts by Pirate supporters and school officials to remove the flag failed.

The rivalry ended when Berea High and Berea Foundation were merged in 1968 and became Berea Community.

COMMUNITIES AND SCHOOLS

Fred Engle

This is a column about a selected, non-comprehensive group of Madison County communities and schools. College Hill was the second name for the community in northeastern Madison County. It was first scornfully called "Texas," after Alber Oldham rode over the ground of Nathan Lipscombe's 2,700-acre property in 1843. He said it was so sorry he wouldn't even have it as a gift. After the Civil War, two communities in Kentucky were found to have the name of Texas, and our Texas became College Hill. This new name was chosen because of the school located there.

Nearby Waco was named in 1847 by Phil Huffman, who ran a pottery in the area and liked the existing Waco, Texas. This Texas name came from the Hueco Indians. The area has excellent clay. A pottery was destroyed by Confederate cavalry during the Civil War, but other potteries have prospered in the area. Kirksville was first called Centerville, but the name was changed in 1845 to honor store owner Samuel Kirkenball. Nearby Round Hill is named for the pre-Indian mound found there. Valley View's name is self-evident and was chosen in 1891 by J.H. Powell and S.F. Rock. A booming lumber mill business existed there in the early twentieth century. The Valley View ferry is said to be the oldest business in Kentucky, founded in 1780 and still in operation today.

The first merchant in Kingston was Theodore King (hence the name). The post office opened in 1846 and, for many years, there was a Masonic Lodge there. The old road from Richmond to Berea used to take a ninety-degree turn to the right in Kingston. The highway now bypasses Elliston, named for Thomas Ellis, a mill operator located there in 1848. Brassfield was named by D.G. Martin for his grandmother. Early store owner Pat Doyle passed on his name to Doylesville.

Dozens of log and then frame one-room schools existed in the early days of the county for grade school students. In 1908, an act of legislature authorized county school boards to establish high schools in each county. These high schools actually served grades 1–12. County high schools began with Waco and Kirksville (1912), followed by Union City (1913), Newby and Speedwell (1919), then Red House and White Hall (1921). Valley View merged with Miller in 1924. Bobtown (1928) started as a high school and then became a junior high in 1933.

In 1934, a program of consolidation was begun for the high schools of the county. A new state requirement said that an accredited high school should have an enrollment of at least a hundred pupils. Since no high school in the county met this requirement, consolidation was necessary. In 1939, the buildings were completed, and the existing small high schools were consolidated into four. Waco, Kingston and Kirksville were expanded, and the newly built Central High School was located outside of Richmond. In 1956, the consolidation advocates won again and Waco, Kingston and Kirksville lost their high schools—all replaced by Madison Central.

The consolidation dampened the community spirit in many areas throughout the county. Without a basketball team to band them together, something was lost. The high schools were the center of the community and although consolidation helped provide better laboratories and save resources, these small communities were forever changed.

BUSINESSES

CRAFTSMEN AND TRADESMEN LINED RICHMOND STREETS IN THE 1800S

Robert Grise

From the notebooks kept by newspaper editor French Tipton, we can learn something about the earliest merchants and craftsmen in Richmond.

In the early 1800s, Richmond was a small county seat village of about 250 citizens. In the center of a grid of unimproved dirt (or mud) and rock streets sat the first courthouse in Richmond. There were about fifty residences in the village, only a few of which were made of stone or brick. Tipton wrote that Thomas Howard, who came from Lexington, was the first significant merchant here.

Opposite the public square were a number of one-story buildings (some of them made of log), which housed stores, taverns and craftsmen, such as saddle and harness makers, shoemakers, hatters, cabinetmakers and repairers of firearms. Three or four blacksmiths were on Irvine Street and other places at the edge of town. Nearly everything the Richmond citizens used was grown, processed or produced locally.

Around 1830, fine furniture was made by John Lawrence, Hugh Goodin and James N. Crutcher. David Chevis specialized in making chairs that could handle rough wear in settlers' cabins. Wool and fur hats were made by Thomas Boyd, Hiram Doolin, Jacob Miller and Frederick Miller, the father of U.S. Supreme Court Justice Samuel Freeman Miller. Several tailors practiced their skills in the block of First Street, opposite the courthouse.

Businesses

On Water Street, originally named South Street, George Brown and Joseph Lees had a large wool-carding factory powered by a steam engine. A lot of Madison County farms had sheep back then, and many farming women used their own wool to weave cloth and then make winter clothes for the family. Lees was also said to have spent considerable time trying to invent a perpetual motion machine, but of course, he never succeeded. Other buildings on South Street were mostly stables and storehouses for businesses on Main Street.

Saddles, bridles and harnesses were made by Charles C. Porter and Thomas G. Little. Boots and shoes were handmade for Madison Countians by William Dean, Sam Freeman, Milbon Rayburn and David Rowland, the grandfather of David Francis, who became governor of Missouri. In the low place on Irvine Street, first called North Street, beside Dreaming Creek, Samuel Logan operated a tannery of nearly a hundred vats. His business produced a large volume of leather for the boot, harness and saddle trades and what surely was a considerable amount of offensive odors.

Main Street Richmond was a center of commerce in 1901. This photo depicts storefronts, merchants and infrastructure conditions around the turn of the century.

Up on Main Street, John McKee had a long "rope walk" on which handmade rope (usually of hemp) was made by having workers walk along a suspended rope, adding one strand at a time. On the First Christian Church corner of West Main and Lancaster was the Shackelford iron factory, where horseshoes, axes, hoes, hinges, nails, plows and carriage hardware were made for those early settlers.

INTERESTING ENTERPRISES

Robert Grise

Some interesting businesses operated in Richmond at the end of the nineteenth century. Among them were a carriage works, a barrel factory and an electric light company.

A few years after the end of the Civil War, John Donelson opened a carriage sales business on Main Street in Richmond, conveniently located next door to Fox's Livery Stable. As the sale of buggies, carriages, carts and wagons increased, Donelson decided that he could make his own vehicles with as good quality as those he had been importing from distant cities and sell them at a lower price since he would not have to pay the freight to ship them.

Donelson built a large two-story frame building at the southwest corner of South Second and Water Streets and hired a number of experienced craftsmen. They soon began turning out well-designed buggies, which were constructed and decorated according to the preferences of the buyers. He used locally produced materials such as seasoned hardwood, leather and hardware made by a local iron factory and Madison County blacksmiths, thus contributing to the local economy in a number of ways. The Donelson Carriage Works earned an excellent reputation not only for its buggies but also for its sturdy and dependable carts and wagons. The business flourished during the 1880s and '90s but went into decline with the arrival of the automobile in the early 1900s.

In the 1890s, a barrel factory, the Hume Cooperage Company, was established by the Hume family on a four-acre site at the end of Estill Avenue at Irvine Street. It was said that a number of loggers up the Kentucky River were kept busy all year long cutting oak logs, which were cut up into 18,000 barrel staves a day. The factory had a log cutting and seasoning area, a milling department (which cut and shaped the staves with steam) and an assembly factory. For a number of years, there were about 200 employees who could produce up to 1,000 barrels a day.

In Richmond from 1874 on, gas was used for lighting, including streetlights. About 2:00 a.m. on the morning of November 12, 1898, the Richmond Gas Works at the Dreaming Creek crossing on East Main exploded. A local newspaper reported that residents were awakened by a noise that "sounded like a load of coal was dumped down the front stairs." The fire bell rang constantly, there was confusion in the streets and it was reported that persons gathered at a couple of local churches, thinking that the end of the world had occurred.

Something had to be done, for the gas streetlights were no longer operating and there was no gas for residence lighting or cooking. In 1899, an out-of-town company obtained city council approval to build an electric light plant on Laurel Street, one block from the Richmond, Nicholasville, Irvine, & Beattyville Railroad (Riney-B) depot. A large brick building was constructed and a steam powered generator of less than 100 kilowatts was installed on Main Street, and many residences were signed up for the service.

Unfortunately, financial troubles plagued the company and it went into receivership. It was reorganized, and more capital was raised. The two organizers of the company were indicted. Still the lights did not come on. The editor of the Richmond newspaper, the *Climax*, wrote in disgust that "Richmond will have electricity when she is struck by lightning."

After several unsuccessful attempts to operate the enterprise, Judge Scott ordered the plant sold in May 1900. It was bought by Stanton B. Hume, who promised that the power would be on by January 1901.

RICHMOND'S DOWNTOWN DRUGSTORES

Robert Grise

From post-Civil War times up to the 1970s, there were nearly always three or four drugstores in downtown Richmond. The names changed over the years, but the locations remained more or less the same.

In our column, old newspapers and other local history works, there are many descriptions of old drugstores in Madison County's past. Griggs's, Collins's and Perry's Drugstores served Madison County in the first half of the twentieth century.

A lot of older folks remember Begley's, which was established by Robert Begley after World War II in the old drugstore building at the corner of

Main and North Second Streets, the site of the previous Herndon and (later) Hagan & Herndon store.

When Begley's closed in the 1960s, it was the ending of a hundred years of dispensing medications in that same building. Over the years the Richmond-based Begley Corporation grew to include a lot of Begley drugstores. It has since been sold to the Rite Aid chain.

According to several sources, such as old Richmond newspapers and French Tipton's notebooks, R.W. White (or a predecessor) started his drugstore in 1828 in a building at the corner of Main and South First Streets. He became best known for his patented children's worm medicine "White's Cream Vermifuge," which he sold to a patented medicine corporation with national distribution. White also invented several other medications, a common practice among druggists back then.

After some years, White took in a partner, and the drugstore became Ballard & White. The store was later known as Ballard, White & Francis. After World

The Hinkle brothers' drugstore was located at the corner of East Main and Madison Streets. The Hinkles constructed the first building in Richmond built specifically as a pharmacy, drugstore and "short order" soda fountain. The authors remember Hinkle's excellent deserts, including one quite rich and fancy banana split called the "College Widow."

War I, Joe T. Griggs bought the place, and it was Griggs's Drugstore for about twenty years. Oren Collins became the owner sometime around 1940. For over 150 uninterrupted years, that drugstore was a popular meeting place, especially on court days on First Street and on Saturdays, when folks from the county came into town to sell and buy animals and crops and do some shopping.

In 1885, W.G. White opened his drugstore at 221 West Main Street. In 1898, it became Perry and Thomas. Then, Henry L. Perry, who had been an employee of White, bought out his late partner's interest after Thomas died in 1909. In addition to the prescription medications and patent medicines for just about any ailment, Perry had a popular soda fountain with ice creams that were advertised as being made from "the purest cream that can be bought." It was known as Perry's Drugstore until about 1940, when it closed.

We older folks remember from our younger days the soda fountains at Cornett's, (later Byrd) in the corner of the Glyndon Hotel; Stockton's, a popular teenage after school hangout in the 1940s (located on West Main between the two Jett & Hall stores); and the Hinkle drugstore.

THE GLYNDON HOTEL AT THE TURN OF THE TWENTIETH CENTURY

Robert Grise

The Glyndon Hotel, that imposing five-story brick building on the corner of West Main and South Third Streets, has served Richmond's visitors for over 120 years. The hotel was originally constructed on that corner in 1889, replacing the old opera house, which had to be closed when the brick back wall became so unstable that people became afraid to attend performances there. According to old illustrations, the first Glyndon Hotel building was a rather high-style brick structure compared to its somewhat plain replacement, the present building. During most of those early years G.W. Willis was the manager.

On September 26, 1889, a grand opening ball was held in the ballroom that was regularly used as the hotel dining room. The committee organizing the festivities for this largest building in downtown Richmond included O.H. Chenault, W.S. Hume, E.T. Burnam, Waller Bennett, G.W. Phelps, W.B. Bright and H.L. Perry, all leading citizens in the county.

The Glyndon was the biggest, finest hotel in Richmond. Guest rooms were lighted by gaslights and heated by fireplaces and stoves. Water was drawn

This 1939 photo shows the lower level of the Glyndon Hotel with its downtown storefront. The hotel's name is Danish and means "Haven of Rest." The building continued to operate as a hotel until recently.

from three large cisterns behind the building, and there were bathrooms on every floor. In addition to regular meal service, lavish dinners were served for special occasions in the ballroom/dining room, and many a formal dance and wedding reception was held there.

The first hotel building was so badly burned in a fire on May 22, 1891, that the entire structure had to be torn down. A new building, the present one, was soon erected and opened in the fall of 1892. It had a long promenade porch that ran along the entire length of the building on Third Street in order to give ladies a safe and somewhat secluded place to stroll.

G.G. Corzelius became the manager of the new hotel, and he presided over it for twenty-seven years. During that time, many famous politicians and speakers of national reputation stayed at the Glyndon. Unfortunately, over the years the place began to get somewhat run down, with furniture getting worn, beds sagging and wallpaper yellowing. Plumbing problems became more frequent and the first system of electric lights became inadequate.

On Saturday, March 8, 1919, Corzelius closed the hotel and held a two-day sale of furnishings in preparation for giving up management on April 1. Traveling salesmen and other visitors accustomed to staying at Glyndon, especially those arriving on evening trains, had some difficulty in obtaining other lodging on short notice.

C.C. Rhodus, a Richmond native, leased the hotel and became the new manager. He ordered new equipment and many new fixtures, but there were delays in receiving furniture shipments, and his hope of reopening the hotel promptly was not realized. A few weeks later it was reopened with the promise that extensive remodeling would take place during the next year. Hot water would accompany the cold throughout the building, steam heat would be installed, and a number of guest rooms would actually have private bathrooms. New equipment would be installed in the kitchen and other new services would be offered. "Richmond has long needed a hotel with these modern improvements," a *Richmond Daily Register* article stated, "and it will be a source of pleasure to the many people who make Richmond in their itinerary."

AN ASSORTMENT OF LOCAL BUSINESSES

Robert Grise

Three interesting businesses that existed in Richmond in the early years of the twentieth century were the Grand Opera House, the Ida May Coal Company and Stanifer's clothing store.

The Grand Opera House was a popular place of amusement for Madison Countians back then. It was included in the Gus Sun Circuit, a vaudeville booking agent for some 216 theatres. In its advertisements, the opera house stated that Gus Sun provided "only the highest class of refined vaudeville acts." Short "moving pictures" on non-flammable film were accompanied by appropriate music. A typical evening's fare consisted of two vaudeville acts, two short motion pictures and a song by a professional vaudeville performer, or perhaps a local person, illustrated by several painted picture slides. One popular performance was the sad "Father, Dear Father, Come Home with Me Now," with several slides of a little girl trying to get her father out of the saloon.

The vaudeville acts were changed three times a week, and at least one of the motion pictures was new each night. In 1910, manager W.P. Baxter stated to the *Richmond Climax* that his opera house received the patronage of the leading citizens of Richmond because it had "high-class, clean entertainments, with no objectionable features being permitted under any circumstances," and it was therefore, "a safe and proper place for ladies and children to attend, whether accompanied by escorts or guardians or not." And, of course, in those days there were no performances on Sunday. Admission for both adults and children was a mere ten cents!

Some traveling drama troupes were booked through the National Theatre Owners' Association of New York City, thus providing local citizens a chance to see some of the same entertainment that had been produced in that great city. A person could find out what was playing that evening by calling 412, the telephone number of the opera house office at 109 East Main Street.

The Ida May Coal Company had its office and storage yard at the L&A Railroad crossing on North Third Street. It provided coal at retail for hundreds of fireplaces and coal stoves in Richmond and Madison County and at wholesale for large consumers, such as Caldwell School on North Second and several small manufacturing firms. Some enterprising persons bought wagonloads of coal at wholesale prices and traveled the streets of Richmond, selling it by the bushel to homeowners.

Ida May Coal was mined near Beattyville and brought by rail directly to the two-acre storage yard, in which 2,500 tons could be stored at one time. In addition, the firm also sold a high quality coal obtained from Monarch Coal Company in the Black Mountains of Virginia and a lower-cost coal mined southeast of Richmond by the Big Hill Coal Company. Several laborers were hired to work in the storage yard, and a number of drivers of company wagons made the deliveries.

J.S. Stanifer's clothing store on the corner of West Main and Second Streets was the ancestor of the present Jett & Hall at that location. Established at another location in Richmond in 1906 with the name of Stanifer and Soper, the store proved successful. In September 1909, Stanifer became the sole owner and, in January 1910, he moved the store to its longtime location on West Main.

Stanifer carried the better brands of men's and boys' clothing in those days, but the brand names are largely unfamiliar to us: David Adler suits, Montague and Gibson hats, Just-Rite shoes for men, Clewett shirts and Arrow celluloid shirt collars (which were separate items in those days). Stanifer's also had a merchant tailor department in which a man could have a suit made to order, if he didn't find a ready-made one that pleased him. Shoes sold for around $3 to $6, and Adler brand wool suits ranged from $5 to $20.

MILLS HAVE BECOME A THING OF THE PAST

Fred Engle

Many mills of different types have existed throughout the history of Madison County. French Tipton recorded that the first commercial mill was Hamm's Mill, which began operation in 1786. Others were Carpenter's (1788), Hawkins's and Cochran's, both on Silver Creek (1790s), Leech's at Paint Lick and Halley's on Otter Creek (1795). Later came Douglas's Mill on Muddy Creek. There is a historical marker along Barnes Mill Road where Barnes's Mill once stood.

J.L. Sowers wrote in the *Richmond Daily Register*, in 1937, about gristmills on Silver Creek called Bogie's, Hagan's and Moran's. There was a mill boy with a sack for the shorts and another one for the middlings. You often had to wait all day for your turn at the mill.

Other mills in Madison County's past include Pott's Old Steam Mill on Paint Lick Creek, Stone House Mill at the mouth of Silver Creek, Oggs's Mill on Muddy Creek and Miller's Old Steam Mill on Tates Creek. Weddles Mill at Doylesville burned in 1971.

The Barlow Planing Mill was established in Richmond between East Main and Water Streets, next to Collins Street, around 1885. Nearly twenty years later, in 1904, the business was bought by the Soper family and renamed the Richmond Lumber Company.

From their office at 358 East Main, the Soper family presided over a 210-foot-wide area on Main Street, running back along Collins Street some 275 feet to Water Street. In addition to the usual lumberyard materials (such as rough and dressed lumber, doors, windows, moldings and builders' hardware), they also carried such things as lime, cement, plaster lath and animal hair for making plaster. This lumberyard went out of business during the Depression.

One of the biggest mills in Madison County was built at Valley View by G.A. Roy in 1891. Called the Southern Lumber Company, it had a three-story-high band saw with wheels twelve feet in diameter. About four miles of booms were constructed on the river to catch logs, which had been purchased upstream and then floated down the river. At a daily rate of 250 logs, the mill cut 30 million board feet of lumber annually. The ground floor of the mill had three boilers, which provided steam for two massive steam engines that powered all the mill's machinery. Logs were floated down the Kentucky River to Valley View, cut up and shipped via the Richmond, Nicholasville, Irvine, & Beattyville Railroad.

By 1898, the Southern Lumber Company had built some forty tenant houses and two bridges over Tates Creek. It also had its own steam plant, electric power and light generator and telephone system. In the 1930s, the decline of the railroad, the scarcity of good timber, and the Depression brought an end to the business.

This postcard of the J.W. Zaring Grain & Mill Company advertised Zaring's Patent Flour, with the slogan, "This is the Best That's Made." The mill also produced cornmeal and marketed throughout Kentucky and nearby states.

My mother used to send me over the hill to the gristmill on North Street near Third Street in Richmond to get fresh ground cornmeal. It made mighty good cornbread. But the largest mill I personally remember was the Zaring Mill in downtown Richmond, built on the banks of Dreaming Creek. A CVS drugstore now occupies that location. It was six stories high and was established in 1892 by J.W. Zaring. The location on East Main had previously housed Potts Bonanza Mills. Zaring died in 1917, and the mill was run by his son, Allen. Allen Zaring sold the business in 1947 to G.G. Vernon, Morris Cox and Chester Luxon. In 1954, the final product rolled off the conveyer belt and the mill ground to a halt. The old mill was torn down in 1955 to make way for an expanding Kroger store.

Mills have been a part of our heritage for many years but, in Madison County, they are now a thing of the past.

Four Richmond Mills

Robert Grise

Lumber and grain mills were essential businesses in the early 1900s, providing wood for housing and grinding grains for people and livestock. Four early Richmond mills were the Stafford's Planing Mill, the Carse Lumber Company, the Blanton-Congleton Lumber Company and the East End Mills.

Stafford's Planing Mill was built by Frank Stafford in 1879, on Richmond's Irvine Street next to Dreaming Creek, where a tannery operated in pioneer days. The planing mill building was eighty-five feet long and forty-seven feet wide. A work force of several men and boys operated machinery that made window sashes, shutters, doors, facings and other such milled wood products.

Power for Stafford's Mill was furnished by a steam engine with a 12-inch bore and a 42-inch stroke. The 28-foot-long boiler burned the scrap wood and sent the smoke up a 75-foot-high smoke pipe. The first floor had a large ripsaw, a 500-pound grindstone and a large planer that could turn out 10,000 feet of flooring a day. The second floor had a whole host of small machines (gougers, shapers and punchers) that were run by belts from the overhead power drive and turned out finished products. Several fires during the next quarter century burned their stock and their building, finally forcing the closing of the mill.

Back around 1890, A.E. Carse, a Michigan businessman, started a lumber and hardware business at the corner of East Main and Orchard Street in

Richmond, where Hicks Lumber Company is now located. He not only sold lumber from eastern Kentucky but also hardware, roofing and paint for the building trade in Richmond.

Deliveries were made by horse and long-bed wagons, specially built for the hauling of long pieces of lumber. Back in those days, there were still a lot of large, solid "first growth" trees to be cut and sent down the Kentucky River to sawmills at such places as Ford and Valley View. Railroads also brought lumber to Richmond.

Under the name of Ed Blanton and Company, W.E. Blanton of Richmond started a lumberyard in 1903, on North Third Street at the RNI&B Railroad. The business thrived and soon, Captain J.R. Pates, former conductor on the old RNI&B Railroad, became a partner. In 1910, with several partners, the firm was incorporated under the name Blanton-Congleton Lumber Company.

After the incorporation, a drying kiln for green lumber and a shed that would hold 125,000 feet of flooring were built. The planing mill was two stories high, with sidings, moldings and tobacco hogsheads made on the first floor and window frames on the second. The business, which covered two city blocks, also carried window sashes, doors, mantels, wood shingles and roofing. Lumber in wholesale carload lots was shipped to surrounding towns. Around 1910, this lumberyard hired about twenty full-time workers.

In the days before World War I, Sanders and Schooler advertised that their East End Mills could turn out 75 barrels of flour and 600 bushels of cornmeal a day. Their three-story-high mill building, which was located adjacent to the railroad tracks on Irvine Street in Richmond, was built of brick, wood and tin siding. The steam-driven machinery was all brand new when the mill was built by brothers J.B. and S.D. Sanders in November 1909. In June of the following year, R.C. Schooler bought a third interest in the mill.

In those early days of the twentieth century, Sanders and Schooler bought wheat from local farmers and produced a number of grades of flour, including Sanders's Special White Rose, Perfection Purity, Blue Bell and Mary. These flours were sold to many grocery stores in Madison and surrounding counties. Sanders and Schooler also ground cornmeal and livestock feed for folks in the county. An attached warehouse could hold 20,000 bushels before it was processed at the mill.

The Waco Pottery

Fred Engle

Many are familiar with Bybee Pottery, owned by the Cornelison family. The pottery's intricate, hand-made pieces have been made by generations of Cornelisons and have been sold all over the country. It is the only major pottery remaining in the eastern part of the county that was once riddled with potteries, taking advantage of the rich clay soil in the area. Another important pottery was the Waco Pottery. I remember it from a field trip in grade school when we visited both potteries, which were close by.

A pottery operated in Waco before the Civil War. Its owner was Valentine Baumstark. Another pottery, operated by Dennis Zittle, was located across the road. Zittle later worked for Baumstark. Around 1900 the property was sold to George W. Grinstead, who made stoneware, brick and tile. A few years later John M. Cockrell, Grinstead's stepson, and E.B. Stone formed a partnership, took over the business, and named it the Waco Pottery. A second kiln was built from brick fired by the original pre-Civil War kiln.

The purpose of the second kiln was to produce art pottery, which became quite famous. After being dug, transported and ground, the clay was weighed

Clay used at the Waco Pottery was dug from the nearby Grinstead farm by hand with pick and shovel, then hauled by wagon and team about one mile to the pottery. It was then chopped and ground in a mill, using horse power. The clay was stored in large size bundles in a cool, damp storage room until ready for use. This 1906 photo shows John Baumstark and employees with a team of mules in front of the pottery.

so that each designed piece would be uniform in size, then the clay was beaten together (a process called boxing balls) to beat out air pockets. E.B. Stone and Dean Stone were the potters who turned the wheels and shaped the clay by hand into various pieces. Cockrell assisted them. Each piece was fired in the kiln twice. After the first firing, it was called bisque. Then it was glazed and fired a second time. Coal was hauled in to fire the kilns. The pottery thus made was quite expensive.

Many varied pieces were made: dishes, plates, cups, saucers, sugar bowls, cream pitchers and water pitchers of all sizes. Vases were popular and large ones were made on special order. There were many colors to choose from. Deep blues and greens were popular, but pastels and matte colors were also used. Most famous of all was the "strawberry" color, which ranged from a light tan with dark edges to a very dark maroon, depending on the placement in the kiln. This color has never really been duplicated, so if you have a "strawberry" piece from the Waco Pottery, you have a collector's item. The art pottery was shipped all over the Appalachian area, bought by Berea College and sold direct to tourists. Although the art pottery made Waco famous, the firm continued to turn out tile and brick at the original kiln.

The death of Stone in 1942 and the disruption by World War II caused the art division to close in 1946. Cockrell continued to turn out farm drain tile until his death in 1969. Bricks from the art pottery kiln (torn down in the '60s) went into a fireplace and chimney at the home of Mrs. Lois Easterling, John Cockrell's daughter. The bricks were fired by her father and made from clay from her grandmother's farm. I am indebted to Mrs. Easterling for information about the Waco Pottery, another piece of Madison's past.

BOONE TAVERN OPENED IN 1909

Fred Engle

Many people have eaten at Boone Tavern in downtown Berea, and more have spent the night there. Most of these guests probably did not realize that the hotel was opened back in the fall of 1909.

At that time it was on the main north-south road, dusty old U.S. 25, nicknamed the Dixie Highway. The hotel was only two stories and there were twenty-five rooms under the flat roof. It has always been owned and operated by Berea College. Its original purpose was to house guests of the

Berea's historic Boone Tavern quickly became a tourist destination along the Dixie Highway. A few of the famous people who have stayed at Boone Tavern over the years include Bruce Barton, Louis Bromfield, Pearl Buck, Henry Ford, Robert Frost, Charles F. Kettering, Eleanor Roosevelt and Thorton Wilder.

college. Woodburning stoves and coal oil lamps provided heat and light for guests, and the furniture was handmade by Berea College students.

It proved such a popular place that another story was added in 1910. An old picture of Boone Tavern in 1910 showed a horse trough in front of the building, awnings and no pillars on the U.S. 25 side. The streets were dirt and the only vehicle in the picture was a buggy. The horse pulling the buggy was at the filling station—the trough.

Then, as now, students worked as clerks and waitresses. Much of the food was produced by the college farm. The farm produced enough eggs, bread and milk to market these items all over Madison County. As the inn grew, the spaces over the adjoining stores became additional rooms for guests.

In 1928, an annex was built on Short Street, and the dining room and lobby were expanded. A gift shop was also opened at this time to display and sell products made by students.

In 1959, a million dollar renovation took place, putting a bath in each room and installing complete air conditioning. The Georgian dining room was enlarged to seat 200, while the Oak Room grew to handle 100 guests for parties and meetings. Sixty-seven guest rooms were made available, nearly three times the original.

The most recent renovation of the historic hotel and restaurant was completed in 2009. The over $11 million renovation brought many updates and modern conveniences to the building, while preserving the history and integrity of this important part of Madison's heritage.

THE *RICHMOND DAILY REGISTER* AND OTHER LOCAL NEWSPAPERS

Fred Engle

On December 1, 1917, the *Richmond Daily Register* rolled off its First Street presses for the first time. It was the product of owner-publisher Shelton M. Saufley Sr., who had, in March of 1917, purchased the *Kentucky Register* and the weekly *Climax-Madisonian*, which was the combination of two previous newspapers. The *Richmond Daily Register* became Madison County's first daily newspaper.

This circa 1930 photo shows *Richmond Daily Register* staff outside their office building. Pictured are (front row, left to right) Ben Chenault, Willis Mores, Ernest Wiggins and Edgar Wiggins, (back row, left to right) Howard "Peck" Paynter, Duke Gordon, Jack Park, Mrs. T.T. Covington, Cleo Dixon, Shelton Saufley Sr. and Roger Pickels.

Saufley was editor-publisher of the *Stanford Interior Journal* from 1910 to 1917. A Democrat, he was active in state politics, serving as state representative and insurance commissioner. He was a member of the First Baptist Church and the Knights of Phythias.

Keen Johnson bought a half interest in the *Daily Register* in 1925 and became its editor. He later became Lieutenant Governor (1935) and then Governor of Kentucky (1939). Other partners in earlier days were Shelton M. Saufley Jr. and T.B. Challinor. Editors of the paper (besides the two Saufleys and Johnson) have included James A. Miller Jr. (1939–1944), Miss Vera Gillespie (1944–45) and Randall Fields (1966–1977). Reverend John Cobb published a column of news from the African American community from 1918 to 1958. Several editors have served the paper in the past few decades, including the current editor Bill Robinson, who also served as editor from 1978 to 1984.

The *Daily Register* had only published a short time in its original place on North First Street (across from the courthouse) before moving to the building built especially to house it on South Second. The *Daily Register* moved its offices to its current location in the old Coca-Cola building on Big Hill Avenue in 1978. It still seems strange to me to drive down the hill from Main to Water and see no newsprint, no paperboys, no reporters. Today, Shelton Saufley Sr. would have to hunt to find his newspaper.

Also in 1978, the paper dropped "Daily" from its name, becoming the *Richmond Register*. The *Register* still publishes local and national news, although the presses of today are far advanced over the 1917 system. Linotype is gone, and computer programs have replaced older newspaper technologies.

Many other papers have existed in Richmond since the 1809 establishment of the *Globe or Universal Register*. Other old Richmond papers and their founding dates include the *Luminary* (1810), *Farmers Chronicle* (1822), *Richmond Republican* (1822), *Whig Chronicle* (1845), *Weekly Messenger* (1852), *Kentucky Register* (1866), *Climax* (1887), *Semiweekly Pantagraph* (1894) and *Madisonian* (1913). Some of these papers lasted a short time, some a long time. Many were continuations of earlier papers that changed owners and names. The *Kentucky Rebel*, *Mountain Boomer* and *Mountain Democrat* were very short duration publications, which appeared toward the end of the Civil War. Central University, Eastern and Berea College have also produced student newspapers through the years.

The first newspaper in Berea was the *Reporter*, which stopped publication when the *Citizen* was started in 1899. The *Citizen* changed its name to the *Berea Citizen* in 1958 and continues to provide weekly news to Berea residents.

The *Berea Evangelist*, a more or less semi-monthly paper which dealt largely with religious matters, was started in 1884. A weekly publication, the *Berea News*, was founded in 1906 but moved to London in 1908. Another *Berea News* operated for about a year around 1930.

EARLY TRAVEL IN MADISON COUNTY

Robert Grise

Running up and down the interstate and zipping around the bypass in our modern automobiles, we are likely to forget how different travel was in Madison County's past. Whether walking or taking a ferry, stagecoach, horse, car or bus, early travel was rough.

In the 1800s, main roads were mostly private turnpikes paved with loose rock (more or less), which had tollhouses at which the traveler had to "pay up" soon after he left the Richmond city limits. The roads were scarcely

In the 1800s, people walked or went by horse—which was not a whole lot faster than walking. Folks didn't travel far; lots of residents of Madison County lived all their lives without ever crossing the county line. This photo from the French Tipton Papers shows seven people and a goat on a wire suspension bridge over Paint Lick Creek near Kirksville.

The first ferry in Madison was that of Richard Calloway at Boonesborough in 1775. This picture shows the Boonesborough Ferry and Boonesborough Bridge. Other early ferries were on Jack's Creek in 1785, on Silver Creek and Mill Run in 1786, and at the mouth of Paint Lick Creek in 1789. Stone's (later Clay's) ferry was established in 1792 on the Kentucky River. Valley View Ferry, which crosses the Kentucky River, was established in 1780 and is still in operation.

an improvement over the trails of the Indians and the pioneers. The county roads were dirt tracks, and there were very few bridges. Streams were usually forded and passengers sometimes had to get out of a heavily loaded wagon or coach in order for the horses to be able to pull the vehicle up the steep bank on the other side of the stream. There were no road maps, no numbered highway signs, nor signs telling the mileage to the next towns. A person going on a long trip had to stop every so often along the way to ask directions.

In the 1880s, the Lexington, Richmond, & Irvine ten-passenger stagecoach arrived at the Garnett House opposite the courthouse on Second Street in Richmond three times a day. Originally called the "Idee House," the fifty-room hotel started in 1871. In December 1875, the heirs of I.D. Smith sold the building to J.R. Garnett, who operated the hotel under the new name. In addition to passengers, the arriving stagecoaches carried packages, special "rush items," and the U.S. mail. It was said that the appearance of the stagecoach was one of the highlights of the day in Richmond over a hundred years ago.

Three agents and three drivers were the total personnel for the stagecoach company, which had been started in 1838 by Thomas H. Hume of Lexington and joined by William W. Pigg of Richmond in 1866. The "rolling stock" consisted of three large stagecoaches and twenty-four horses. The fare from Richmond to either Lexington or Irvine was $1.50 one way.

In the early 1900s, Azbill's Livery Stable rented horses and "stylish rigs for all occasions." Azbill's and a number of other stables rented space for vehicles and fed horses for private owners in addition to running a freight wagon service.

The first auto to appear in Richmond was probably that of a Lexington patent medicine salesman in 1900. A bus line that lasted only one week was started in 1906. The fourteen-passenger bus took passengers to Lexington, which took two hours and nineteen minutes, and the fare was $1.85 for the round trip. The steep, sharp curve at Clay's Ferry was the bus line's undoing. In the 1920s the Consolidated Coach Corporation operated buses through Richmond. During a flood in 1926, passengers were ferried by rowboat across the river at Clay's Ferry to buses on the other side.

THE ROWLAND BRANCH OF THE L&N

Robert Grise

The first railroad to Richmond was the Rowland Branch of the L&N, built soon after the end of the Civil War. It entered the city from the southwest, taking the same route that our modern tracks do today. After a $750,000 bond issue was narrowly approved by the voters of the county in 1867, the L&N started construction of the 33 miles of track from Rowland near Stanford through Lancaster and Paint Lick to Richmond, where it "dead-ended" at a turntable between East Main and Irvine Streets, where the freight yards are now located. The first train ran on November 8, 1868.

For many years there were two trains a day, running at speeds ranging from 10 to 25 miles per hour. The locomotives were the 4-6-0 type, with three drive wheels on each side and a large smokestack through which the exhaust steam was released in order to increase the draft through the firebox.

In addition to its tender, the locomotive usually pulled one passenger car, two or three freight cars, occasionally a livestock car and a caboose.

The trains from Richmond stopped at Fort Estill, Duncannon, Silver Creek and Paint Lick before leaving the county, going through two tunnels to Lancaster and then on to Rowland, where trains could be caught for Louisville or Knoxville.

In 1882, the Kentucky Central Railroad built a line south from Cincinnati through Winchester to where the L&N Rowland Branch track ended in Richmond, making direct transportation to northern cities possible. The KC also leased the two miles of L&N track from Richmond to Fort Estill, allowing KC trains to run south to Berea, Corbin and Livingston. This arrangement lasted until 1890 when the L&N bought the Kentucky Central, making it all one system.

Around the turn of the century, there were sixteen L&N passenger trains a day through Richmond! At various times, such as court days and the beginning and end of school terms, the passenger station on East Main handled between 300 and 400 travelers. Also in the early 1900s, Irvine Street

This photo from the 1960s shows local historian Jonathan T. Dorris standing along the L&N railroad tracks in Richmond. Railroads have been an important part of Madison's heritage since the 1800s.

was frequently crowded with droves of cattle and mules headed for the stock pens awaiting loading onto railroad stock cars.

The Rowland Branch became unprofitable in the 1920s, and the tracks were taken up in the early 1930s. The old roadbed can still be seen today at several points on Highway 52 between Richmond and Paint Lick.

THE SELLS BROTHERS CIRCUS TRAIN DISASTER

Robert Grise

When a circus train wrecked over 100 years ago, lions, tigers, elephants and all sorts of other unusual animals from foreign countries ran loose for a while near Paint Lick. Some say there are still some unusual looking wild birds in that area.

If you say, "But there's no railroad through Paint Lick," you are right; however, there used to be one. The Rowland Branch of the L&N railroad was built in 1868, just a few years after the end of Civil War. It ran from an L&N junction about eight miles south of Lancaster, then through Lancaster, Paint Lick, Silver Creek village and Fort Estill, ending up in Richmond at the little freight yard between East Main and Irvine Streets. In 1882, the Kentucky Central railroad was built from Cincinnati and cut through Richmond. The KC leased the Rowland Branch from 1882 to 1890, making it possible for trains to run from Cincinnati through Richmond and Paint Lick and on to Lancaster.

Dr. J.R. Kinnaird of Lancaster was the L&N physician in 1882. Fortunately for us, in 1926, he wrote an account of the circus train wreck in the L&N magazine entitled "My First Experience with the L&N."

Kinnaird wrote that in August 1882, the Sells Brothers Circus had performances in Richmond. After being loaded on their railroad cars, the circus was headed on to London via Lancaster during the night.

After a long, hard pull up to Moran's Summit, the highest point on the Rowland Branch, the train ran down the grade toward Paint Lick at an alarmingly increasing rate. A coupling broke, dividing the train. In those days, there were no air brakes on railroad cars. Just before the train reached the bridge over Paint Lick Creek, the engineer discovered that the train was divided and, for some inexplicable reason, slowed the front section. The inevitable crash of the rear section into the front occurred.

The first four or five cars remained on the track, but all the rest were smashed, derailed and rolled over the steep embankment at the edge of the creek. Kinnaird wrote that the sight of "the dead and dying, the howls of wild animals, the confusion in the dark, the cries of dazed men and women made an everlasting impression upon all those who witnessed the scene."

The locomotive was sent on to Lancaster to bring physicians back. Finally, when all was under control, it was found that most of the wild animals were captured, three persons had been killed and about twenty were injured.

THE "RINEY-B" RAILROAD

Robert Grise

In 1890, a railroad that ran through Madison County was organized to carry freight, raw materials and passengers between Versailles, Nicholasville, Valley View, Richmond, Irvine and Beattyville. It was named the Richmond, Nicholasville, Irvine and Beattyville Railroad. From its initials, it developed the nickname "Riney-B."

Coming from Nicholasville, the single-track railroad entered Madison County crossing over the Kentucky River at Valley View on a high bridge that had S-shaped approaches. The old bridge supports are still visible from the ferry crossing. From that river crossing, the railroad ran up Tates Creek to Million and then on to Richmond, generally following the north side of Tates Creek Road for several miles. It circled up around the east side of the Arlington estate, crossing under the Lexington Road and going around the north end of the city. Four mixed passenger and freight trains stopped each day at the station on North Third Street. From there, the Riney-B ran east, crossing Four Mile Road just next to the old Four Mile Cemetery.

After leaving the Richmond station the rails ran on to Moberly, Brassfield and Panola before crossing the county line and going on to Irvine and Beattyville. The railroad at first carried distillery supplies to and from Versailles, logs and lumber to and from Valley View and coal from Beattyville. Two passenger trains a day ran in both directions.

The railroad did not do well financially, mainly because it ran east and west where there was not nearly the volume of traffic as flowed north and south on the already established big railroads. The enterprise went bankrupt and was forced into receivership in December 1891. In 1897, under a foreclosure order, the RNI&B was sold to a new group of investors. It was reorganized under the name Louisville & Atlantic Railroad, even though it

This photo from the French Tipton Papers shows the tracks of the Riney-B railroad running alongside Tates Creek Road. Goggins Lane is seen running perpendicular to the tracks at the right side of the picture. At the top of the hill, a man is standing at the site of Kit Carson's birthplace.

never got closer to Louisville than about seventy-five miles and it was several hundred miles from the Atlantic shore!

In 1909, the L&N acquired the L&A and it became a section of "the Old Reliable." In a few years, the L&N gave up on it and built a new line directly from Winchester to Beattyville. On October 3, 1932, in the midst of the Great Depression, the L&N announced that the last passenger train on the RNI&B section had run on September 30, 1932. Thus ended an enterprise that lasted from 1890 to 1932.

Evidences of the old railroad bed can still be seen along Tates Creek Road near Goggins Lane and at the tunnel between Million and the river. If you want to actually drive along the old roadbed, go out the Irvine Road (Highway 52) and turn left onto Charlie Norris Road. Turn either way at the first intersection, now called Moberly No. 1 Road, and you will be moving down the same roadbed that the old steam locomotives did over a century ago.

DEVORE'S LARGE TRANSPORTATION BUSINESS

Robert Grise

At the beginning of the twentieth century, William Devore had quite a transportation empire locally. Known by many as "Uncle Billy," Devore operated out of a large livery stable at the end of Irvine Street at Church Street in Richmond.

Devore bought the livery stable from Jake Collins, a local furniture dealer and undertaker. Collins built the livery stable in 1890 with oak and poplar lumber from Valley View, in order to have a place to shelter his expensive black hearses and handsome black horses that pulled the hearses. Devore paid Collins $3,000 for the stable buildings in 1893, and it became the headquarters for his horse and buggy, transfer wagon and omnibus business for a third of a century.

At that time Richmond was having something of a boom. The L&N had more than fifteen trains a day, and the RNI&B also had trains from Nicholasville and Beattyville stopping at the station on North Third Street. Devore met all those trains with his omnibus, carrying passengers and freight to the Glyndon Hotel, the Garnett House on Second Street, stores and houses. Devore's omnibus was a long sturdy wagon drawn by four strong horses. It had seats for a number of persons and load space for large trunks, suitcases and packages.

The Richmond Street Railway Company was organized in 1890. Small streetcars with open sides were pulled by mules on tracks running from the L&N passenger station on East Main up to the Glyndon Hotel corner, where they turned and ran out North Third Street to the RNI&B passenger station. The fare was five cents. In 1902, Devore bought the company from local businessmen and added that transportation system to his "empire." Unfortunately, the Richmond folks did not take to the streetcars as expected and the venture lasted only a few years.

Through the years, Devore's Richmond Transfer Company's horse-drawn transfer wagon, horse and buggy and omnibus enterprise had less and less business as folks bought their own automobiles and businesses got their own trucks. Finally in the 1920s, the horses stood idle and the wagons and buggies gathered dust.

MADISON COUNTY LIFE

RICHMOND'S DOWNTOWN CHURCHES

Fred Engle

The histories of many churches in Richmond have been written up on different occasions in Madison's Heritage. Here is information on some downtown church buildings, lasting symbols of the importance of religion in the history of Madison County.

A Baptist church occupied the corner of West Main and Lancaster from 1828 until 2004 when the First Baptist Church congregation moved to a new building on the Eastern Bypass. The first religious group at the Main Street location was the Particular Baptists. The land was given to them by General Green Clay in 1828 and a one-story wooden structure was erected in 1830. In 1882, the Missionary Baptist Church and the Regular Baptist Church built a new facility, jointly owned by the two groups at the corner. In 1908, the name of the congregation was changed to First Baptist Church as the Missionary group bought out the non-missionary group. The last church building on the corner downtown was built in the Classical Revival style in 1922 and dedicated on May 11, 1924.

The First Presbyterian Church was organized in 1827, and a building went up the next year. The current structure is the third and dates to 1921. It is Gothic Revival style, and its major feature is the central tower. Most Presbyterian churches have a similar tower, and it goes back to the denomination's beginnings in Scotland. The state Church of Scotland is Presbyterian, and St. Giles Cathedral on High Street in Edinburgh is the

This photo shows the 1939 congregation of the First Baptist Church gathered in front of the building's main entrance at the corner of Main Street and Lancaster Avenue. Dr. Robert Sory and Pastor J. Edward Hewlett are at the far left. A young Fred Engle is seen wearing a hat near the top left, his mother at the center and his father at the far right, in front of the church sign.

mother church of Presbyterianism. Inside the local building is a beautiful wooden hammer-beam truss across an oak-lined ceiling.

The First Methodist Church began in 1833, on the northwest corner of Second and Irvine Streets. In 1841, a frame building was constructed and, in 1881, a new brick church was built. It is still standing and now houses businesses. The present edifice, which houses the First United Methodist Church, was completed in 1927 at Main and Church Streets and is also of the Classical Revival style. Its columns are Corinthian; First Baptist's were Doric and, before it burned, First Christian's were Ionic.

The building that housed the Christ Episcopal Church is the oldest church house in Richmond dating to June 19, 1887. The Episcopalians began in Richmond as a mission located at the corner of West Main Street and Tates Creek Avenue in 1871. The stained glass windows were imported from Europe and are beautiful. The building now houses the Richmond Area Arts Council, and a congregation has recently started meeting in the old church house.

The Disciples of Christ denomination organized in Richmond in 1844 and originally worshiped where the Federal Building now stands. They soon moved across the street and built a wooden building at their present location at the Corner of Main and Lancaster. It burned in 1855. A third building was constructed in 1913 of the same Classical Revival style used by the Methodists and Baptists. It burned in 1959 and was replaced by the present magnificent building, completed and dedicated in 1962.

The Roman Catholics operated in Madison County from its early days via traveling priests from Bardstown and Lexington. In 1856, mission stations were opened in Richmond, Rogersville and Boonesborough. In 1865, a small frame church was built on West Main Street and was under the Winchester parish. In 1906, the Catholic Church burned and the present stone edifice was constructed in 1908. It was the first stone church in town. St. Mark's purchased additional land in 1953 and opened an elementary school in the 1960s.

So, if anyone asks you the ages of Main Street's downtown churches, you can give them the correct answer.

OLD MADISON COUNTY CHURCHES

Fred Engle

It is nearly impossible to write about all the churches that have existed in Madison County over the years. Here are a few that have been a part of Madison County life for many decades.

There have been hundreds of Baptist Churches throughout the history of the county. Two Baptist churches were organized in Richmond in 1828. The Missionary Baptists organized in 1867, drawing its members from county congregations. They met at Green's Opera House and then began to share the Regular Baptist building on Main Street in 1882, alternating Sundays. In 1908, the Missionary group bought out the non-missionary group and the church became known as First Baptist.

Out of the First Missionary Baptist Church have come five others: Calvary, Broadway, Rosedale, Linden Street and White Hall. Calvary and Rosedale began with tent meetings, Broadway with a tobacco warehouse revival. First Baptist has been faithful to its missionary commitment.

There is another church by the name of First Baptist Church in Richmond, founded in 1844 to serve blacks of that faith. Known over time by several other names, the church at the corner of Francis and Collins Streets was at one time housed in a brick building built in 1860. In 1921, a new building was constructed and, in 1994, the current building replaced the 1921 structure, keeping its stained glass windows and bell.

The African Methodist Episcopal Church, now known as St. Paul AME, was organized in Richmond in 1872. The congregation first met in a boxcar on the L&N Railroad tracks and then met in a log cabin on Water Street and Madison Avenue until 1874, when they moved to Hill Street. In 1903, the AME built a church at Francis and E Streets, where the present edifice was later erected in 1927.

The first Methodist church in Madison County was Proctor's Chapel, near Boonesborough (1790). The church was moved and the name changed to Providence Methodist Church but ceased to exist with the coming of Red House Methodist Church. In 1796, other Methodist churches in the county were Green's Chapel, Muddy Creek, Irvine and Concord. None of these churches are the oldest. Squire Boone was a Baptist. The first organized Baptist Church in the county was the Tates Creek or Republican Baptist, which was organized around 1783. They were Regular Baptists. The Separate Baptists began at Otter Creek Church in 1786. Viney Fork Baptist Church at Speedwell was founded in 1797. The Old Cane Springs Baptist Church was organized near College Hill in 1803, the Union City Baptist in 1812.

The Union Church in Berea is one of the most famous churches in Madison County. Tracing its history back to John G. Fee, the current church building was dedicated in 1922. *Photo courtesy of Berea Community Collection, Historical Collections, Berea College, Berea, KY.*

Some other interesting church histories written about in Madison's Heritage articles include Mt. Zion Christian Church, White Oak Pond Christian Church, Immanuel Baptist Church, Gilead Baptist Church, Bethlehem Baptist Church, Wallaceton Baptist Church, Waco Baptist Church, Drowning Creek Baptist Church, Bethel Christian Church and Tates Creek Baptist Church. Information on these and many other churches in the county may be found on the Madison's Heritage website.

PATTIE A. CLAY: A LASTING MEMORIAL

Fred A. Engle

Newcomers to our county may wonder about the name of the Richmond hospital. Here is the story.

Brutus J. Clay II was the son of Cassius M. Clay of White Hall. Born in 1847, he received an engineering degree from the University of Michigan. In 1905, President Theodore Roosevelt appointed him Minister to Switzerland. His first wife was Pattie Amelia Field.

This circa 1900 photo of the Pattie A. Clay Infirmary shows nurses and the old building on Glyndon Avenue. The infirmary featured a ward for African American patients.

Mrs. Pattie Field Clay died in 1891 and, in 1893, her husband made available a property on Glyndon Avenue, facing North Third Street, as the location of Richmond's first hospital to be known as the Pattie A. Clay Infirmary. The building was previously owned by James P. Herndon.

Prior to this, the only place for the sick to go was the home of a Mrs. Grayson on Water Street. For a dollar a day she provided bed and board for the seriously ill. Mrs. Sam Bennett Jr., Miss Belle Bennett, Mrs. Green Clay, Mrs. Fannie Park Smith and Mrs. Susan Baldwin Jason had been pushing for a public hospital, and Brutus J. Clay provided the means.

After some remodeling, the Pattie A. Clay Infirmary opened for business in the brick house on Glyndon Avenue. It remained on Glyndon Avenue until its move to the present bypass location in 1970. There were originally six private rooms and a ward. The Board of Directors consisted of women, mainly representatives from local churches.

In 1927, the hospital was expanded at a cost of $75,000. Forty beds were available after the expansion. The hospital boasted three doctors, a furnished and equipped laboratory and operating rooms. The doctors were M.M. Robinson, J.A. Arbuckle and B.F. Robinson. In 1939, hospital capacity was raised to forty-five. More remodeling took place in 1945. Miss Elizabeth Scott was the longtime hospital superintendent, and Mrs. George D. Simmons served many years as treasurer.

Other hospitals in Richmond have included the Gibson Hospital on West Main Street, the Pope Hospital on North Second Street and the trachoma hospital at the Irvinton estate. Berea College had a hospital, and Eastern staffed an infirmary. In the early 1900s, there was a small hospital for black patients on First Street.

And that is a short version of the origins of the Pattie A. Clay Hospital—a critical part of Madison's heritage.

THE GIBSON HOSPITAL WAS FOUNDED BY PHYSICIAN BROTHERS

Fred Engle

The Gibson Hospital was founded at the turn of the twentieth century by Dr. Hugh Renfro Gibson and his brother, Dr. Wade Moss Gibson.

Hugh Gibson graduated from Nashville's Vanderbilt University School of Medicine in 1888. Then he went to Vienna, Austria (the medical Mecca of the world at that time) for post-graduate study in medicine and surgery. He returned from Vienna and came to Madison County to practice medicine, with a lifelong dream of having his own hospital.

Moss Gibson graduated from Louisville's Hospital College of Medicine in 1897 and came to Richmond, entering into a partnership with his brother. Together they bought the old Ezekiel Field house at the corner of West Main and Fifth Streets to use as their hospital. Field was a member of Daniel Boone's party that settled the Boonesborough area. Built in 1818, the home had two bedrooms, a living room, dining room and a hall on the first floor, with a large dirt floor kitchen in the basement. The joists of the kitchen were hand-hewn logs, made from huge trees, two feet square and twenty feet long. A large walk-in fireplace of native stone was built at one end of the kitchen where all the cooking was done. The inside and outside walls of the original house were eighteen inches thick.

The doors were Christian doors, the upper part forming a cross, the lower panel forming an open book, the Bible. The glass for the windows was handblown and came from Philadelphia by oxcart. At the time the house was built, Fifth Street was called Lyman Street. While the building was still a residence, additions were made upstairs, including two tower rooms, a porch and columns.

The hospital began with five bedrooms for patients. In 1908, ten new rooms were added.

A nephew of the two founders, Dr. Shelby Gibson Carr, inherited the Gibson Hospital in 1935. A wing containing twenty patients' rooms, a new kitchen, sterilizing equipment and a nurses' dining room was added on the Fifth Street side.

In 1946, sixteen more patient rooms, as well as X-ray and laboratory rooms, were added. A home for the nursing staff was built in the back of the hospital. Additional rooms were added in 1955 and 1964. The new X-ray machine, installed in 1964, was the first electronically-controlled machine of that kind in a Kentucky hospital and was made by General Electric.

Dr. Carr died in 1968 and the hospital closed soon after. The heirs sold the building and the 150-year-old Ezekiel Field house was torn down. A filling station is now at that site on West Main and Fifth. My thanks to EKU librarian Jerry Dimitrov for much of the above information.

Thus, the Gibson brothers realized their dream and provided efficient medical service to the people of Madison County.

IRVINTON: ELIZABETH IRVINE'S GIFT TO RICHMOND

Robert Grise

When warm weather brings crowds to the Irvine-McDowell City Park in Richmond for ballgames, picnics, family reunions and school and church group events, these activities are actually against the desires of the old Southern lady who left the place to the city many years ago.

Mrs. Elizabeth S. Irvine wrote in her will in 1915 that "it is my will that there be no public gatherings, such as fairs, chautauquas, picnics, shows or crowds to collect in the Irvinton grounds."

Mrs. Irvine was the daughter of the well-known pioneer Colonel David Irvine and Susannah McDowell Irvine, the eldest child of Dr. Ephriam McDowell of Danville, the famous surgeon. In 1846, she married her first cousin, William M. Irvine, and they lived at Irvinton, the big old house in the middle of what is now the city park. The house was originally built in the early 1820s by Dr. Anthony Wayne Rollins and sold in 1829 to Colonel David Irvine who made additions to the building.

Mrs. Irvine's handwritten and unwitnessed will was composed in June 1915. In this twenty-nine page document, she bequeathed the Irvinton estate, "which lies between the streets in Richmond now called Fourth Avenue [Lancaster Avenue] and Second Street...to the Kentucky Medical Society... to be called forever the Irvine and McDowell (Ephriam) Memorial." She wrote that "if the Irvine and McDowell Memorial should ever languish... under the control of the Medical Society of Kentucky... [that would] cause the Irvinton estate to revert to the city of Richmond as a public park."

Mrs. Irvine, who was widowed in 1897, had seven children, all of whom died in infancy, except one daughter, Bessie, who lived to the age of eighteen before dying of typhoid fever. Mrs. Irvine lived alone in the old mansion with a number of servants to care for the place until she died in 1920.

After her death, the house with its valuable furnishings and land went to the Kentucky Medical Society. A thirty-two-bed hospital operated at Irvinton between October 1926 and November 1950, under the direction of Dr. Robert Sory, serving patients from eastern Kentucky who suffered from the eye disease trachoma. Many of the furnishings were stolen from the house after Mrs. Irvine's death and other items went missing in the 1950s when the trachoma hospital ceased to operate.

Mrs. Irvine's will had many requirements for the use of the estate, first as a hospital and then as a public park. A large granite monument honoring

David Irvine, Dr. McDowell, William Irvine and her daughter, Bessie D. Irvine, was to be erected in front of the house. A stone with an inscription identifying the house as "The Irvine and McDowell Memorial" was to be placed above the front door. Just about every room in the house was specified as a memorial to some particular member of her family.

The restrictions ran on for many pages and included some that are now unconstitutional. When used as a hospital, there were to be no soldiers as patients or nurses in training. "It is my will," she wrote, "that this devise is exclusively for white patients, no colored or foreigners." She especially disliked school people. She wrote, "Irvinton shall never by gift or sale be in any way connected with or used by the Eastern Normal School...or any other institution of learning."

In the 1920s and, again in the 1950s and early '60s, there were many lengthy legal struggles through the courts in order for the city to finally get title to the property and declare many of the will restrictions unconstitutional or illegal and to develop the park to its present excellent state, open to all citizens.

The Irvinton estate once housed a trachoma hospital and a public library. It is now the home of the Richmond Visitor's Center and features a museum. Many festivals and events are held throughout the year at the Irvine-McDowell Park.

The Beginnings of the Blue Grass Army Depot

Robert Grise

The Blue Grass Ordnance Depot, the place where those dangerous and troublesome nerve gas bombs are now stored, was first established in 1941, just after the Japanese attack on Pearl Harbor and the United States' entry into World War II.

The depot was established under the Statutory Authority Title II of the First War Power Act of December 18, 1941, Public Law 354 of the 77th U.S. Congress. President Roosevelt issued executive order 9001, which sped the law into application on the 27th day of that December.

The first step was to acquire the necessary 14,599 acres of choice Madison County farmland, which was next to the major north–south U.S. Highway 25 and the main line of the L&N Railroad. Some of the landowners were disturbed when the government attempted to buy their land at the value that the farmers had listed for taxation purposes, resulting in some court battles. The village of Kavanaugh and other named neighborhoods, churches, houses and cemeteries were completely removed, and many county roads closed.

Construction of the depot began after the commanding officer arrived on April 25, 1942. Enough civilian workers were hired by the last of May that actual construction work was started. It was so easy to get a job there and so easy to earn overtime pay that many persons who had survived the long miserable 1930s financial depression referred to the depot as "the money orchard."

Administrative buildings, maintenance buildings, railroad sidings and "igloos" for the storage of ammunitions in one section of the depot were completed, so that the area could be turned over to the U.S. Army Ordnance Department on September 4, 1942. On the second day of October, actual daily operations began with the arrival of seven railroad carloads of ammunition.

The depot was operated by the U.S. Government until October 2 of the following year, when control was assumed by Blue Grass Ordnance Depot, Incorporated, a subsidiary of the Firestone Tire and Rubber Company, which operated the place on a "cost plus fee" basis. Construction had essentially been completed by then, and most employees unloaded and loaded the ammunition, worked in maintenance or were involved in the necessary paperwork. During the summer of 1943, when the U.S. involvement in the war was so intense, there were 3,800 people employed and dozens of railroad carloads of ammunition were handled daily.

On October 25, 1945, the army once again took over control. From 1946 until 1950, there was relative peace for the U.S., and the number of depot employees decreased through attrition and layoffs. At the beginning of the Korean War in July 1950, there were only about 1,000 civilian employees. With the U.S. entry into the war, the number of employees quickly increased to about 3,000. By 1960, when everything was peaceful again, there were about 675 regular civilian employees and seven U.S. Army commissioned officers.

The Blue Grass Ordnance Depot was renamed the Blue Grass Army Depot on August 1, 1962, and placed under the control of the Ammunition Procurement & Supply Agency in Joliet, Illinois.

RECOLLECTIONS OF SPEEDWELL

Fred Engle

My thanks to Opal Gentry, Mr. and Mrs. Tom Hocker, Fay Broughton and Jean Turner for providing information, upon which much of this article on Speedwell is based. Mrs. Gentry was my contact, and she gathered the material for me.

On March 1, 1899, an article by Governor Ed Brown on various places in Madison County appeared in the *Richmond Climax*, including a section on Speedwell:

> *Speedwell is located in a beautiful country ten miles from the city. It has a good school house, blacksmith shop, two or three stores, two churches, Christian and Baptist. Viney Fork meeting house is one of the oldest in the county. Some of our best citizens are from this locality, for instance Henry Dillingham, Clay Broaddus, Pleas Broaddus, and ex-Representative John Speed Smith...Dr. Brownlee Oldham is located in this village. Squire Hendren and William West are the principal farmers in this section, as are Budd Todd, George Todd, Mr. Gilbert, and Sam Deatherage—known as Big Sam. Near this place was the former home of our most popular coal merchant, Merritt Harber.*

Captain Crook, a Revolutionary War hero, was buried near Speedwell along the Crooksville Road, which was named in his honor. Soon other pioneers settled, including Christopher Harris. Viney Fork Baptist Church was established in 1797, Harris being the first pastor. The sandstone building is still standing.

No one knows exactly how Speedwell got its name, but there were many wild plants called speedwell growing in the area. Speedwell is a tiny ground cover common in Kentucky with blue racemes of flowers. This photograph from the French Tipton Papers shows the Speedwell community as it was in the nineteenth century.

Arnold Fritz started school at Speedwell in 1930. He was there when mobster and bank robber John Dillinger came through the area, scaring them all. The road was gravel. Fritz drank his first bottle of pop at the store, paying two cents. Speedwell High School existed until 1934. After that, high school students were bused to Kingston and Waco. The Speedwell grade school remained until the Blue Grass Ordnance Depot came, forcing many families to move from the area.

The coming of the Ordnance took roughly 15,000 acres, about half of the Speedwell community. The churches lost half their active membership and many old farms and houses belonging to the Raybourn, Harris, Halcomb, Fritz, Drew and Golden families were taken. New subdivisions have opened in recent years, rebuilding the population of the area.

Mr. and Mrs. Tom Hocker lived in the community for ninety years. At one time, there were two groceries. One was owned by James Hendricks, before being sold to Oscar Gentry, whose wife Opal operated the store for many years. Bill West owned the other store and also ran the post office. Both are closed now. The gristmill was run by Shelby Powell and Tom Hocker. The old high school building burned down. Speedwell had three doctors, Dr. R.C. Coomer, Dr. Harry Hendricks and Dr. Giles Harris. Dr. Coomer only had one arm, losing the other in a hunting accident. He visited patients via horse and buggy, being particularly busy during the World War I flu epidemic. His wife raised chickens and turkeys. Early establishments included the Crooksville gristmill, a saloon, the Matt Lakes furniture store, the small Collins grocery, a haberdashery and post office in a general store. The post office, started in 1852. In 1873, Aliza Venable was the post master, then W.J. Powell, then Shelby and Georgia Powell. The railroad went through Brassfield, two miles from Speedwell. There also existed the Independent Order of Odd Fellows Lodge, No. 1295, Speedwell.

This then is Speedwell, once a thriving Madison County community, then in decline, now growing again and alive in the memories of many Madison Countians.

EARLE COMBS: YANKEE CENTER FIELDER

Fred Engle

Earle Combs, center fielder for the New York Yankees, was born in Owsley County, Kentucky. He played baseball for teams in local coal mining towns. He enrolled at Eastern when he was seventeen. His first year playing for the Maroons was 1918, and he batted .596.

In 1922, he signed a contract to play for the Louisville Colonels of the American Association. Joe McCarthy was the team's manager that year. Combs batted .344 and, the next year, he batted .380. The New York Yankees signed him for $50,000 (this was before there was such a thing as a minimum wage in the U.S., so the equivalent spending power today is in the multimillion dollar category). His first year was 1924. He played center field between Bob Meusel and Babe Ruth. Later that year he broke his leg. Even so, he played all of 1925, batting .342. His first World Series was in 1926. He played in a total of nine World Series with the Yankees. He played in four World Series (series, not individual games) during his career without making any errors.

The 1927 New York Yankees team remains the greatest team in the history of the game. Ruth hit sixty home runs, Combs batted .356 and they and Lou Gehrig were part of "murderer's row."

This 1931 photo shows baseball great Earle Combs sporting an Eastern sweater, standing on the old athletic field behind the University Building. After Combs's amazing career, he served on the EKU Board of Regents and had a dormitory on Eastern's campus and a field at the Irvine-McDowell Park named in his honor. He is also a member of the Madison County Historical Society's Heritage Walk of Fame and was honored with a plaque in front of the courthouse.

There was no warning track in the outfields back then. On July 24, 1934, Combs, concentrating on catching a long fly ball, crashed into the wall. He injured his skull, his shoulder and his knee. He recovered from his injuries and returned to center field the next year. However, a collision with another outfielder injured his shoulder again. He decided to quit playing while he was ahead. His replacement for the Yankees was Joe DiMaggio. Combs stayed on with the Yankees organization until 1943. He later was on the staff of three other major league teams.

Combs returned to Madison County where he raised beef cattle on his farm. He was selected for the Baseball Hall of Fame in 1970. I was lucky enough to be one of 800 who paid tribute to the man at a ceremony at Eastern on March 10, 1970.

I first knew Mr. Combs in 1945. The Madison-Model baseball team went to the state tournament finals in both 1945 and 1946. Mr. Combs's son, Charles, was a member of both teams. He was a year older than I. My job was scorekeeper, and I was beginning my longstanding relationship with the *Richmond Daily Register* (over sixty-five years now, on and off), writing up high school sports.

Bob Ackman was the official coach, but Mr. Combs was on the bench helping coach (along with Mr. Harold Moberly) the Purple Nine. I always thought that was million-dollar coaching for free. Mr. Combs had two other sons—Earle Jr. and Donald (Donald was later an outstanding swimming coach at Eastern).

Mr. Combs never used his fame to boost himself above others. Over the years, when we met he always greeted me with "Hello, Fred. Good to see you." His amazing life is a unique part of Madison's heritage.

SPIDER THURMAN AND ROY KIDD: MADISON'S HALL OF FAMERS

Fred Engle

Two men with Madison County ties were among twenty-six charter members inducted into the Dawahares Kentucky High School Athletic Association Hall of Fame in 1988. The local men were James Wyatt "Spider" Thurman and Roy Kidd.

Spider Thurman got his nickname when he was in the second grade at Benham in Harlan County. His eyes were swollen shut and the doctor said he must have had a spider bite. Ever since then he was called Spider.

After playing football and basketball at Benham High, he went on to Eastern in the 1930s. There he played football, basketball and ran track and graduated in 1941. He was a Little All-American quarterback for the Maroons and captain of the All-KIAC (Kentucky Intercollegiate Athletic Conference) team. Back then all state schools except Kentucky played in the KIAC.

In 1950, he went to Manchester to coach the Clay County Tigers. The school had never been to the state tournament, and the thirteenth region was usually represented by Harlan or Corbin. During Thurman's eleven years as coach, Clay County won six regionals. In 1961, Thurman came to Eastern as director of alumni affairs, staying until his retirement in 1983.

Roy Kidd was an outstanding player at Corbin High before coming to quarterback Eastern's eleven from 1950 to 1953. He coached the fabulous teams at Madison-Model High School between 1956 and 1961. The Purples, led by Talbott Todd and Freddie Ballou, were exciting to watch.

Kidd's Royal Purples had a record of 54–11–1, won 27 in a row, had 15 consecutive shutouts and were so good that opponents got the Model

This 1968 photo shows Eastern head coach Roy Kidd talking to quarterback Jim Guice during a game at the old Hanger Stadium. Kidd was active in local football for over fifty years. Eastern's football stadium is named in honor of his accomplishments as a player and coach.

division separated from the Madison division. In 1961, when the Madison-Model merger ended, Model no longer had a football team, and Kidd coached Madison High. The Purples were ranked first in the state and Kidd was Coach of the Year.

Kidd became head coach at Eastern in 1964 after serving as assistant coach at Morehead in 1962 and Eastern in 1963. Kidd retired in 2002 with a record of 314–124–8, a .713 winning percentage. Eastern won the national titles (I-AA) in 1979 and 1982, plus two runners-up. Kidd led the Eastern to 16 OVC titles during his tenure and was inducted into the College Football Hall of Fame in 2003.

Madison's Heritage is proud of Thurman and Kidd—true Hall of Famers.

1940 Eastern Team Unbeaten and Untied

Fred Engle

Eastern's 1940 team was the only undefeated, untied football team in the history of Eastern Kentucky University, until Roy Kidd's 1982 championship squad. The 1941 team came close to extending the 1940 team's record, losing only to Western. The head coach of the Maroons, which they were called at that time, was Rome Rankin. His assistants were Tom Samuels, line coach, and Charles "Turkey" Hughes, freshman coach.

Eastern opened with a 20–0 victory over Illinois State Normal, sparked by two touchdown passes from Wyatt "Spider" Thurman to Charles "Chuck" Schuster. Next came an easy 39–0 win over Arkansas A&M, followed by a 35–0 romp over Northern Illinois. Bert Smith ran sixty yards for a touchdown in this game. King College of Bristol, Tennessee, finally scored on the Maroons, but Eastern won 31–7.

Morehead scored twice against the Eastern defense and led 13–7 at the half, but the Maroons punched in three touchdowns in the second half to claim the "Hawg Rifle" by a 27–13 score. Eastern closed out the season with three smashing victories, 48–7 over Cumberland University of Tennessee, 25–0 over Central Michigan and 48–0 over Bowling Green University of Ohio.

Thurman, quarterback of the 1940 team, was joined by three other young men in what became known as the "Harlan Backfield." Bob Mowat and Joe Bill Siphers were from Thurman's home town of Benham in Harlan County, while Travis "Tater" Combs was from the city of Harlan.

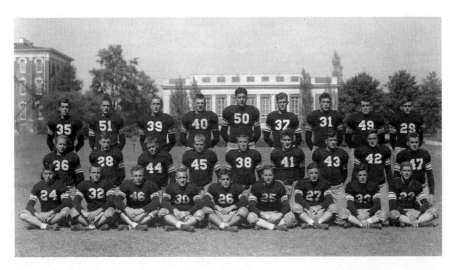

The 1940 undefeated Eastern football team: (front row, left to right) Harold Yinger, Nelson Gordon, Cliff Tinnell, Warren Grob, Bill Cross, Gayle McConnell, Wyatt "Spider" Thurman, George Ordick, Bob Mowat, Al Dressman, Kenneth Perry, (middle row, left to right) Buford Griffith, Bert Smith, Roy Buchaus, Joe Bill Siphers, John Rose, Charles "Chuck" Schuster, Harold White, Walter Mayer, Bill Brown, (back row, left to right) Travis "Tater" Combs, Ber Rasnick, Ted Benedett, Bob Goosens, Francis Haas, Ora Tussey, Larry Lehman, Fred Darling, Ralph Darling, Frank Flanagan, Bill Hickman.

SCHOOL NICKNAMES AND COLORS

Fred Engle

There have been various colors and nicknames of our local schools during my lifetime. My high school and college days were all color oriented. Model students played ball at Madison, using the name Madison-Model. So, I started out with Purples, or to be exact, Royal Purples. Purple and white were the school colors from its beginning in 1920. I attended Madison-Model High from 1943–1947. The Purples had some very good teams during that period, including the baseball team that went to the state tournament finals at Parkway Field in Louisville in 1945 and 1946. Madison Middle School now carries on the purple and white tradition.

Eastern's school colors, maroon and white, were derived from crimson and cream, the athletic team colors of the university's predecessor, Central University, a Southern Presbyterian school. The crimson (maroon) represented the blood of Jesus Christ and the cream (white) was for purity. Eastern's teams were called "Maroons" from the beginning in 1906, along with the name "Normals," until 1963, when they became the "Colonels." *Maroon, White, Fight, Fight!*

When I went to college at Eastern, I joined the Maroons. I never was anything but a color—Purples and then Maroons! Color was also found in

This photo shows the Waco High School Cardinals basketball team and cheerleaders. Many high schools used to exist throughout the county. They competed with each other and with the Richmond and Berea city schools in the district tournament.

other local schools. There were the Central Scarlets, the Kirksville Blue Jays and the Waco Cardinals. Over in Irvine were the Golden Eagles. Schools without color in their nicknames were the Kingston Trojans, Berea High Pirates, Berea Academy-Foundation Lions, Estill County Engineers (from the railroad stops there), Richmond Ramblers and Berea College Mountaineers. When the four county high schools, Central, Waco, Kirksville and Kingston, were merged in 1956, Madison Central took the name Indians. New in the field are the Madison Southern Eagles.

Back in the 1950s and through the early '60s, Coach Roy Kidd's Madison-Model football teams won with regularity, going to the state finals at old Stoll Field in Lexington one year. Jealousy caused defeated opponents to complain and the Kentucky High School Athletic Association broke up the twenty-two year connecting link between the two schools. Model High began fielding separate teams in the midst of the Civil War centennial celebration, including a Battle of Richmond pageant, so they chose the nickname Rebels and used the colors red and gray. During the 1975–1976 school year, the mascot name was changed to the Patriots, and they adopted red, white and blue as their colors.

THE TOBACCO BASEBALL LEAGUE

Fred Engle

In the summer of 1948, I held an invitational baseball tournament for local amateur teams in the area. It was won by the Blue Grass Ordnance Depot team. Around four teams participated in the tournament.

The next spring I organized the Tobacco League as an outgrowth of the tournament. I came up with name because tobacco was a prominent product in the area and foul balls often landed in tobacco fields. Many communities had formal and informal teams that would get together to play in the summer. During the time that the Tobacco League existed, there were also the Legion League, the Bluegrass League and the Central Kentucky League in this area.

I was founder and president of the league, and Julian Shaw was vice-president, succeeding me when I went to the army in 1951. Jim Moberly later ran the league. Original teams in the league included College Hill, Waco, County (Bybee area), Central (Red House/Union City area) and Wildie.

Over the years, many teams participated in the league, including teams from Estill, Fayette, Garrard and Rockastle Counties, in addition to teams from Madison County. Teams included Bearwallow, Berea, Central, Bybee, College Hill, the "County Clippers" from the Bybee area, Ford, Hackley, Kirksville, Lexington, Ravenna, Waco, Wildie and four teams from Richmond—the Lads, Rebels, Redbirds and Tigers. There may have been teams from Lancaster and Paint Lick in 1955.

The league played every Sunday afternoon from around the beginning of May until October 1. Players ranged in age from sixteen to over forty. On average there were five to six teams in the league made up of as many as fifteen to twenty people each. The teams played in several different locations in local communities, including some high school baseball fields. Central played at the Central High School diamond, College Hill had a community diamond, Waco played at Waco High School and Wildie had a community field. Most teams had uniforms, as well as coaches and managers. The league had a printed schedule, complete with advertisements. I wrote up games for the *Richmond Daily Register* covering standings and scores. MVPs were also voted on and trophies came from jeweler Eddie Kessler.

Many teams drew large crowds, particularly for the playoffs, which were held between the top four teams. The winners of the season and playoffs were as follows: 1949 season and playoffs, College Hill, with Central as playoffs runner-up; 1950 season and playoffs, Wildie, with Central as playoffs runner-up; 1951 season, Wildie, playoffs, Central, with College Hill as playoffs runner up; 1952 season, no games played; 1953 season and playoffs, College Hill, with Waco as playoffs runner-up; 1954 season and playoffs, Waco, with College Hill as playoffs runner-up; 1955 season and playoffs, Kirksville, with Waco as playoffs runner-up.

The Tobacco League flourished from 1949 until 1955. Foul balls often landed in tobacco patches, some home runs ended up in ponds. Great fun was had by all and lasting friendships were made.

In 1969, a 20th reunion for the Tobacco Baseball League was held and was followed by a 40th reunion in 1989 and a 50th in 1999. As spring comes every year, Tobacco League members, fewer in number now and not as spry as they were right out of high school, may well pause a moment, look out on the local fields and recall a very special, shared part of Madison's heritage—I know I still remember it all.

HOW WELL DO YOU KNOW LOCAL HISTORY?

Fred Engle

I sometimes like to give quizzes to Madison's Heritage readers. Let's see how you do with these ten questions about Madison County history.

1. Who were the two other girls, besides Daniel Boone's daughter, Jemima, who were captured by Indians while canoeing on the Kentucky River and, besides Squire, what were the names of Daniel's other brothers and sisters?
2. What Indian tribe captured and then adopted Daniel Boone?
3. Who was the first sheriff of Madison County?
4. What was the first African American church in Madison County?

Do you remember "Mozart," the music-loving dog, who, for seventeen years, followed the EKU band onto the football field and students into classes? He is buried on a slope behind the Van Peursem Pavilion on Eastern's campus, with a marker at his grave. Mozart is pictured in this 1960s photo in the Foster Music Building with Eastern President Robert R. Martin.

5. What was name of the region of Madison County in which Berea was established?
6. What was the name of Cassius Clay's anti-slavery newspaper?
7. During the Civil War, what Richmond lady fed John Hunt Morgan's southern troops ham and biscuits one day and Green Clay Smith's northern troops the same meal two days later?
8. Was Madison County named for a former president?
9. For whom were Irvine and Estill County named? What connection did these men have with Madison County?
10. What year did the Foster Band Camp begin?

Let's see how you did:

1. Frances and Elizabeth Calloway. Edward, Samuel, Israel, George, Jonathan, Sarah, Elizabeth, Mary and Hannah
2. The Shawnee
3. Joseph Kennedy (1786–87)
4. Richmond Baptist Church, also known as the United Colored Baptist Church founded in 1844 and pastored by Edmond Martin and Madison Campbell
5. The Glade
6. The *True American*
7. Mrs. Curtis F. Burnam of Burnamwood
8. Admittedly, this one is a bit of a trick question. No, it became a county in 1786 and was named for James Madison, developer of the U.S. Constitution. He did not become president until 1809.
9. Colonel William Irvine and Captain James Estill. Both were early settlers in Madison County (1780s). Estill's Station (Fort Estill) was built in Madison and Irvine was the first clerk of Madison County.
10. 1935. I attended four years (1944–1947). Rehearsals were held under the old Hanger Stadium (about where the Powell building is now), and concerts were every Tuesday, Thursday and Sunday nights in the amphitheater. Then, as now, the last concert ended with the singing of "My Old Kentucky Home."

How did you do? Do you know your Madison County history? If you got them all, then you're a real history buff!

WACO CITIZENS WERE EXCITED ABOUT NEW DIAL TELEPHONE SYSTEM

Robert Grise

The first automatic dial telephone system in this whole section of Kentucky was installed at Waco in Madison County in 1938. Slightly more than 100 subscribers were "cut over" from the old exchange equipment on Thursday, October 12, of that year.

The Waco exchange had for some thirty years consisted of a couple dozen open wire party lines connected to a small switchboard with an operator who could tell the correct time and give advice about such things as how icy and slick the College Hill Road looked at the Waco intersection. Sometimes when a call was made for a person, the operator might say, "I just saw him driving down to the store; do you want me to ring over there?" The operator was also a local news force, spreading word when there was a fire or a death in the community or somebody's cow was out on the road. The country operator could help coordinate when neighbors got together to put a sick person's hay in the barn before it rained.

In those days before the dial made everybody's telephone number a dull four-digit string, most Waco numbers were easy to remember. Goff Adams on College Hill Road, the first subscriber listed in the directory, had the number 48-X. The W.T. Bush General Store was 2, E.A. Bogie was 6-X and Professor J.D. Hamilton was 52-J.

When the automatic system was installed in 1938, there was no longer a Waco operator, and every customer was to dial his or her own connection. And during the first two days, they did just that at a far greater volume than a human operator could ever handle. The *Richmond Daily Register* reported on October 15, 1938, that in the first 31 hours of operation, the Waco and College Hill subscribers dialed up each other over 9,000 times!

Many of the folks had not had much experience with the telephone dial. Some persons got wrong numbers because they did not remove their fingers from the dial wheel as it returned to its normal position. They didn't understand that the actual signaling to the automatic equipment takes place as the wheel returns to rest, not when the finger winds it up to the finger stop. Others dialed "operator" to get Richmond, when the instructions stated that "9" should be dialed. It was reported that one older subscriber misdialed when attempting to call his daughter and demanded to know why some stranger was answering his daughter's phone. A few others reported that there was "this buzzing noise on the line," but that it disappeared when they dialed a number.

The subscribers at Ford got their own dial exchange a few months after Waco got theirs, and the folks in those villages were old experienced hands at operating dial telephones when Richmond finally got its automatic dial telephone system in May 1960, over twenty years later.

REVISITING RURAL RICHMOND

Fred Engle

Richmond has changed a lot in my lifetime. In my youth, it was a very rural town. I grew up at 222 South Third Street. Across the street was a field full of cows. Dreaming Creek flowed between South Second and South Third Streets.

In my area in later years, the Walkers and the Garretts both raised chickens. The Garretts had a milk cow in the barn at the back of our lot. There was a well in their yard. Others raised guineas. At the end of South Third was a stile over the fence, which took you to my father's large vegetable garden. Wade and Tull plowed it in the spring with a team of mules. Afterward, Daddy used a push plow. I gardened too, only under duress. We were digging potatoes on V-J Day. All the whistles, church bells and car horns from Main Street let us know that the long war in the Pacific had finally ended.

Other signs of rural Richmond were the trading of horses and mules in an empty lot on Water Street, the pioneer horse trough sitting in the street, full of water for the thirsty beasts, the human drinking fountain at Owen McKee's, the Zaring Mill at the point where East Main crossed Dreaming Creek, the Soper Saw Mill at Main and Collins, the Patton Blacksmith Shop on North Third and the gristmill on North Street. The city limits were at the corner of Lancaster and Barnes Mill and at Kunkel's filling station on West Main.

A sign of changing times is seen by a drive out Big Hill Avenue. What is missing after a hundred years? The busy tobacco warehouse is gone. There also used to be an empty lot back at the "Y" made by East Main and Big Hill Avenues where the carnivals and circuses set up their tents.

The Madison Country Club used to be just out of town. Across the highway was an empty lot where Madison-Model's baseball team played its home games. The team sometimes used Eastern's diamond where foul balls would break windows in the University Building (Model High back then).

A young Fred Engle and his parents, Kathryn and Dr. Fred A. Engle Sr., sit in front of their home on South Third Street. Both Engle and his coauthor, Robert Grise, grew up in Richmond, fostering lifelong interests in the area's rich history. As witnesses to the many changes in the county over the years and as researchers, teachers and preservers of local memory, they have themselves become parts of Madison's heritage.

Every Saturday on wide North First Street (between Main and Irvine) there was a market. Food, guns, knives and other wares were sold and traded. Singers sang, musicians played and preachers shouted, and it seemed all Madison County walked the sidewalks on Main between Third Street and Madison Avenue. The street was packed from 10:00 a.m. to 8:00 p.m. (when all stores closed, except the drugstores). Every Halloween, Main Street was blocked off from First to Third for the big street fair.

The big entertainment back then was to go out to the depot (pronounced dee-po to differentiate it from the Army deh-po) and watch the trains come in. I remember No. 31 and No. 32. One came north about suppertime, and the other went south about 10:00 p.m. There was a water tower across the tracks from the depot, and the steam engines filled up. The Railway Express office usually had several interesting boxes.

One last memory of rural Richmond: about 1946, I saw for the last time a horse wagon going along West Main Street in front of the First Christian Church—the beginning of the end.

About the Authors and Editor

D r. Engle and Dr. Grise have led remarkably similar lives. Their families have been linked for over eighty years and have become deeply rooted in Madison County. Their fathers taught together at Eastern Kentucky State Teachers College and their mothers also taught in the area. Their children and grandchildren grew up in Richmond. Fred's granddaughter, Kathryn, developed an interest in local history and has worked to continue the efforts of the Madison's Heritage authors.

Dr. Fred A. Engle Jr., Kathryn Engle and Dr. Robert N. Grise pose while attending a banquet in the Keen Johnson Ballroom on Eastern's campus. *Photo by Elizabeth Engle.*

Dr. Engle was born in 1929 and grew up in Richmond. He attended Model starting in 1935 and graduated in 1947. He then enrolled at Eastern and graduated with a BS in both math and commerce in 1951. He was a member of the ROTC and served in the army during the Korean War from 1951 to 1953. He met and married Mary Purves in Edinburgh, Scotland, while in the service. He completed his MBA at the University of Kentucky in 1954. He taught at the College of William and Mary from 1957 to 1959 and then began teaching math and economics courses at Eastern. He received his EdD in higher education foundations from the University of Kentucky in 1966 and retired from teaching at Eastern in 1998 after thirty-nine years of service.

Dr. Grise was born in 1930 in Richmond. He attended Model starting in 1935 and graduated in 1948. He then enrolled at Eastern and graduated with a BA in both English and art in 1952. He was drafted into the army medical corps during the Korean War and served from 1952 to 1954. He married Madison County native Martha Spurlin in August 1954. He received a master's in English education from Eastern in 1955. He taught English and teacher education at Kentucky Wesleyan College from 1955 to 1963 and received his EdD in educational administration from the University of Kentucky in 1963. He began teaching education courses at Eastern starting in 1963 and retired in 1995 after thirty-two years of service.

Kathryn was born in Corbin, Kentucky, in 1989 and grew up in Richmond. She attended Model starting in 1993 and graduated in 2007. She attended Eastern and graduated in 2011 with a BA in English literature, a BBA in general business and a minor in Appalachian Studies. She is currently pursuing a MA in Appalachian Studies at Appalachian State University.